THE
BOOK*of*
NAMES

*Over 1,000 biblical, historical,
and popular names*

Edited by

Sarah M. Peterson

Tyndale House Publishers, Inc.
WHEATON, ILLINOIS

Library of Congress Cataloging-in-Publication Data

The book of names : over 1000 biblical, historical, and popular names / compiled by Sarah
M. Peterson.
   p. cm.
  ISBN 0-8423-0123-2 (softcover)
   1. Names, Personal—Dictionaries. 2. Names in the Bible—Dictionaries. I. Peterson,
Sarah M.
CS2377.B66 1997
929.4'03—DC21   97-5537

Printed in the United States of America

02 01 00 99 98 97
 6   5   4   3   2   1

THE
BOOK *of*
NAMES

CONTENTS

INTRODUCTION

"What are we going to name the baby?"
How do you go about choosing a name?
Since creation, children have been named for

- birth-circumstance (Jacob means "he grasps the heel."
  The Jacob of the Bible was born with his hand
  grasping his twin's heel.)
- a relative or friend
- a quality the parents hoped the child might possess
  (Hope)
- a characteristic of the child
- the appealing sound of a name

The Book of Names is a collection of more than a thousand
names with inspirational meanings and profound histories.
They are names of spiritual significance, whether taken
straight from the Bible or from contemporary culture. Many
of these names are associated with noble and reknowned
people and places.
Each name entry is accompanied by

- identification of the traditional gender associated with
  the name (girl names identified by *italic*, boy names
  by **roman**)—some names are appropriate for either sex
- the ethnic origin of the name
- the meaning of the name

- suggested lifetime Scripture verse, handpicked to reflect the godly meaning and/or heritage of the name
- a short description of the biblical or historical background that makes the name meaningful
- a pronunciation key if needed

The names we give our children are important and lasting gifts. When we identify our children with admirable qualities, special history, and spiritual characteristics, we demonstrate our love for and confidence in the people they are becoming.

BIBLE NAMES

Old Testament Names

*W*ith about twenty-eight hundred names, the Old Testament provides the largest source of biblical names. Names in the Old Testament range from the familiar (David, Rebecca, Daniel, Sarah) to the unusual (Abner, Sherah, Vashti) to the truly weird (Arphaxad, Hoglah).

This compilation of Old Testament names strives to have each name possess two components: (1) The person associated with this name had a positive reputation (i.e., you won't find Cain or Jezebel in this list); and (2) it is a name that would suit a young child, taking into consideration pressures children face during their formative years.

Aaron

Israel's first high priest (Leviticus 8:1-36) and the older brother of Moses (Exodus).
"Enlightened, illumined" (Hebrew)

The LORD is my light and my salvation—so why should I be afraid? The LORD protects me from danger—so why should I tremble? PSALM 27:1

Abel

His offering was accepted by God (Genesis 4:4), but he became the world's first martyr.
"Breath" (Hebrew). Perhaps his name prophetically reflected the shortness of his life.

But I am like an olive tree, thriving in the house of God. I trust in God's unfailing love forever and ever. PSALM 52:8

Abigail

Intelligent and beautiful woman who persuaded David not to kill her foolish husband. Later, Abigail became David's wife (1 Samuel 25).
"Source of delight" (Hebrew)

Take delight in the LORD, and he will give you your heart's desires.
PSALM 37:4

Abner

Saul's military commander who became a strong supporter of David (1, 2 Samuel).
"Father of light" (Hebrew)

I will keep on obeying your law forever and forever. I will walk in freedom, for I have devoted myself to your commandments.
PSALM 119:44, 45

Abraham

He was the father of the Hebrew nation and the ultimate role model for faith (Genesis 12:1-3; 1 Chronicles 1:34; 2:1-2; Hebrews 11:8-10).
"Father of a multitude" (Hebrew)

You welcome those who cheerfully do good, who follow godly ways. But we are not godly. We are constant sinners, so your anger is heavy on us. How can people like us be saved? ISAIAH 64:5

Adam

Adam was the world's first human being, who disobeyed God in the Garden of Eden but was forgiven of his sin and promised a future Savior (Genesis 1–4).
"Man of red earth" (Hebrew). So called because the soil of Palestine from which he, the first man, was created is red.

For we are God's masterpiece. He has created us anew in Christ Jesus, so that we can do the good things he planned for us long ago.
EPHESIANS 2:10

Amasa / *Amasa* UH MAY SUH

Absalom's military leader who helped David after Absalom's death (2 Samuel 17, 19).

"Burden bearer" (Hebrew)

Don't just pretend that you love others. Really love them. Hate what is wrong. Stand on the side of the good. Love each other with genuine affection, and take delight in honoring each other.
ROMANS 12:9-10

Amos AY MUHS

Herdsman who became a prophet and authored the book of Amos.

"Burden bearer" (Hebrew)

Don't just pretend that you love others. Really love them. Hate what is wrong. Stand on the side of the good. Love each other with genuine affection, and take delight in honoring each other.
ROMANS 12:9-10

Amram

Father of Moses, Aaron, and Miriam (Exodus 6:20).

"People exalted" (Hebrew)

When darkness overtakes the godly, light will come bursting in. They are generous, compassionate, and righteous. PSALM 112:4

Asaph AY SAF

He was chief of the Levite musicians appointed by David, and author of twelve psalms (1 Chronicles 6:39; Psalms 50, 73–83).

"Collector, gatherer" (Hebrew)

So, my dear brothers and sisters, be strong and steady, always enthusiastic about the Lord's work, for you know that nothing you do for the Lord is ever useless. 1 CORINTHIANS 15:58

Asher / *Asher*
Jacob's eighth son (Genesis 30:13).
"Happy, blessed" (Hebrew)
I have told you this so that you will be filled with my joy. Yes, your joy will overflow! JOHN 15:11

Baruch BAY ROOK or BEHR UHK
He was Jeremiah's scribe who wrote Jeremiah's prophecies on a parchment and read them in the temple (Jeremiah 32, 36).
"Blessed" (Hebrew)
I have told you this so that you will be filled with my joy. Yes, your joy will overflow! JOHN 15:11

Bathsheba BATH-SHEE BUH
Solomon's mother and one of four women referred to in the New Testament genealogy leading to Christ (2 Samuel 12:24; Matthew 1:6).
"Daughter of an oath" (Hebrew)
Lead me in the right path, O LORD, or my enemies will conquer me. PSALM 5:8

Benaiah / *Benaiah* BEE NIGH UH
He was a brave commander in the armies of both David and Solomon (2 Samuel 8:18; 1 Kings 2:35).
"Jehovah has built" (Hebrew)
God arms me with strength; he has made my way safe.
PSALM 18:32

Benjamin
He was the youngest of Jacob's twelve sons (Genesis 42:13).

"Son of my right hand" (Hebrew)

LORD, don't hold back your tender mercies from me. My only hope is in your unfailing love and faithfulness. PSALM 40:11

Boaz BOH AZ

He married Ruth and became an ancestor of Jesus through David's line (Ruth).
"Fleetness, strength" (Hebrew)

A wise man is mightier than a strong man, and a man of knowledge is more powerful than a strong man. PROVERBS 24:5

Caleb KAY LUHB

He was a faithful partner with Joshua, standing against the evil report of the ten spies (Numbers 13:6-30).
"Bold, impetuous"; or "dog" (Hebrew), signifying faithful affection.

The steps of the godly are directed by the LORD. He delights in every detail of their lives. PSALM 37:23

Cyrus SIGH RUHS

He issued the decree allowing Jews to go back and rebuild Jerusalem (2 Chronicles 36:22-23).
"Sun, throne" (Persian)

The LORD is my light and my salvation—so why should I be afraid? The LORD protects me from danger—so why should I tremble? PSALM 27:1

Why do you like your name?

I like the sound of it and the biblical character. I always took an extra interest in the character of David in the Bible.
David

9

Daniel

This Jewish prophet served as prime minister in Babylon under Nebuchadnezzar and Darius (Daniel 2:48; 6:1-3).
"God is my judge" (Hebrew)

God is my shield, saving those whose hearts are true and right.
PSALM 7:10

Darius DUH RIGH UHS

There are two men by the name of Darius in the Old Testament: (1) The king who was tricked into casting Daniel into the den of lions. He rejoiced in Daniel's salvation and issued a decree ordering all his citizens to consider the almighty God of Daniel (Daniel 6); and (2) The king who ordered the work on the temple in Jerusalem, which had been stopped, to resume (Ezra 6:1-12).
"He who upholds the good" (possibly Persian)

Give me understanding and I will obey your law; I will put it into practice with all my heart. PSALM 119:34

David

He was Israel's greatest king, and author of over half the Psalms (2 Samuel 23:1).
"Beloved" (Hebrew)

Dear friends, let us continue to love one another, for love comes from God. Anyone who loves is born of God and knows God.
1 JOHN 4:7

Deborah

She was a prophetess and judge in the days of the judges and aided Barak in defeating Israel's enemies (Judges 4–5).

"Bee, wasp" (Hebrew). In ancient Egypt, the bee was a symbol of regal power.

Instead, I want to see a mighty flood of justice, a river of righteous living that will never run dry. AMOS 5:24

Dinah DIGH NUH

Dinah was the only recorded daughter of Jacob. She was seduced by a pagan chief's son, which precipitated the massacre of a town by two of her brothers (Genesis 34).
"Judged, avenged" (Hebrew)

Be on guard. Stand true to what you believe. Be courageous. Be strong. 1 CORINTHIANS 16:13

Eldad EL DAD

He was one of the seventy Israelite elders to whom was given the ministry of the Holy Spirit (Numbers 11:25-26).
"God has loved" (Hebrew)

But the LORD still waits for you to come to him so he can show you his love and compassion. For the LORD is a faithful God. Blessed are those who wait for him to help them. ISAIAH 30:18

Eleazar ELEE AY ZUHR

He was Israel's second high priest (Numbers 20:22-29).
"God is Helper" (Hebrew)

God is my shield, saving those whose hearts are true and right. PSALM 7:10

Eli EE LIGH

He was the high priest when Samuel was born and when the

ark of the covenant was captured (1 Samuel 1:17-20; 4:12-18).
"God is high" (Hebrew)

For you bless the godly, O LORD, surrounding them with your shield of love. PSALM 5:12

Elijah IH LIGH JUH
Prophet who defeated his enemies on Mount Carmel and was later caught up into heaven without dying (1, 2 Kings).
"Jehovah is God" (Hebrew)

Once again you will have all the food you want, and you will praise the LORD your God, who does these miracles for you. Never again will my people be disgraced like this. JOEL 2:26

Elisha / *Elisha* IH LIGH SHUH
Successor to Elijah who parted the Jordan and healed Naaman of his leprosy (2 Kings 2:9-14; 5).
"God is Savior" (Hebrew)

O LORD, I have longed for your salvation, and your law is my delight. PSALM 119:174

Enoch EE NUHK
Preacher who was the first of two people recorded in Scripture to leave earth without dying (Genesis 5:24; 2 Kings 2:1-12; Jude 1:14-15).
"Dedicated" (Hebrew)

And I am sure that God, who began the good work within you, will continue his work until it is finally finished on that day when Christ Jesus comes back again. PHILIPPIANS 1:6

Ephraim EE FRA IHM
Joseph's second son (Genesis 41:52).
"Doubly fruitful" (Hebrew)
I long to obey your commandments! Renew my life with your goodness. PSALM 119:40

Esau EE SAW
Jacob's forgiving twin brother, and father of the Edomites (Genesis 25:26; 36:43).
"Hairy" (Hebrew)
Create in me a clean heart, O God. Renew a right spirit within me. PSALM 51:10

Esther ESS TUHR or ESS THUHR
Esther became queen and saved her people, the Jews, from an attempted holocaust (Esther).
"The star" (Can be traced through Hebrew, Latin, and Greek to the Persian, in which it probably signified the planet Venus.)
The LORD is my light and my salvation—so why should I be afraid? The LORD protects me from danger—so why should I tremble? PSALM 27:1

Ethan
A wise man in the time of Solomon (1 Kings 4:31).
"The strong or firm" (Hebrew)
So, my dear brothers and sisters, be strong and steady, always enthusiastic about the Lord's work, for you know that nothing you do for the Lord is ever useless. 1 CORINTHIANS 15:58

Eve

She was history's first woman and the first human to fall to temptation (Genesis 1–2).

"Life, life-giving" (Hebrew)

I long to obey your commandments! Renew my life with your goodness. PSALM 119:40

Ezekiel IH ZEE KIH UHL

Priest and prophet who provided the most complete biblical description of the cherubim and millennial temple (Ezekiel).

"God is strong" (Hebrew)

The Sovereign LORD is my strength! He will make me as surefooted as a deer and bring me safely over the mountains.
HABAKKUK 3:19

Ezra / *Ezra* EZ RUH

Prophet, priest, scribe, and teacher of the Law who led the second (of three) Jewish returns from Persia to Jerusalem (Ezra, Nehemiah).

"Help" (Hebrew)

Live in such a way that God's love can bless you as you wait for the eternal life that our Lord Jesus Christ in his mercy is going to give you. JUDE 1:21

Gabriel / *Gabrielle* GAB BREE EL/GAB BREE EL

Gabriel is one of two angels whom the Bible names (the other is Michael). Gabriel was sent to Mary to tell her she would be the mother of Jesus Christ (Luke 1:26-38).

"God is my strength" (Hebrew)

*The Sovereign LORD is my strength! He will make me as
surefooted as a deer and bring me safely over the mountains.*
HABAKKUK 3:19

Gideon GID EE UHN
An angel commissioned him to raise up an army and defeat
the Midianites (Judges 6–9).
"Great warrior, hewer, feller" (Hebrew)

*Give honor to the LORD, you angels; give honor to the LORD for
his glory and strength.* PSALM 29:1

Hannah HAN UH
She was the godly mother of Samuel (1 Samuel 1).
"Grace, mercy, or prayer" (Hebrew)

*For the LORD God is our light and protector. He gives us grace
and glory. No good thing will the LORD withhold from those who
do what is right.* PSALM 84:11

Hezekiah HEZ IH KIGH UH
He was the king when God saved the city of Jerusalem from
the Assyrians by the death angel (2 Kings 19).
"God is protection" (Hebrew)

*So be strong and take courage, all you who put your hope in the
LORD!* PSALM 31:24

Huldah HUHL DAH
Prophetess in the days of King Josiah who warned of Judah's
downfall (2 Kings 22).
"A weasel or mole" (Hebrew)

Lead me in the right path, O LORD, or my enemies will conquer me. PSALM 5:8

Ira / *Ira* IGH (EYE) RUH
There are two Iras in the Old Testament: (1) David's priest (2 Samuel 20:26); and (2) One of David's heroes (2 Samuel 23:26).
"Descendant" (Hebrew)
The LORD is wonderfully good to those who wait for him and seek him. LAMENTATIONS 3:25

Isaac IGH (EYE) ZIK
He was Abraham's promised son and the father of Jacob (Genesis 17:19; 25:21-26).
"Laughter" (Hebrew)
You will show me the way of life, granting me the joy of your presence and the pleasures of living with you forever.
PSALM 16:11

Isaiah IGH (EYE) ZAY UH
He was the Old Testament's greatest prophet (Isaiah).
"God's salvation" (Hebrew)
I will lift up a cup symbolizing his salvation; I will praise the LORD's name for saving me. PSALM 116:13

Jacob
He fathered twelve sons, who later founded Israel's twelve tribes (Genesis 25–50).
"Following after, supplanter" (Hebrew). The Lord molded Jacob into a man after God's heart.

*Those who lead blameless lives and do what is right, speaking the
truth from sincere hearts. Those who do not charge interest on the
money they lend, and who refuse to accept bribes to testify against
the innocent. Such people will stand firm forever.* PSALM 15:2, 5

Jael / Jael JAY UHL
She killed Sisera, the enemy of Israel, and was praised in a
song by Deborah and Barak (Judges 4–5).
"Chamois" (Hebrew), a small, goatlike antelope

*I will offer you a sacrifice of thanksgiving and call on the name
of the* LORD. PSALM 116:17

Jair JAY UHR
There are three Jairs in the Old Testament: (1) Descendant of
Manasseh who, during the conquest of Jordan under Moses,
took several villages on the border of Bashan and Gilead
(Numbers 32:41); (2) A judge who judged Israel for twenty-
two years (Judges 10:3, 5); and (3) Father of Mordecai
(Esther 2:5).
"He enlightens" (Hebrew)

Reverence for the LORD *is the foundation of true wisdom. The
rewards of wisdom come to all who obey him. Praise his name
forever!* PSALM 111:10

Jared
The father of Enoch (Genesis 5:15-20).
"He who descends" (Hebrew)

Commit everything you do to the LORD. *Trust him, and he will
help you.* PSALM 37:5

17

Japheth JAY FETH
Noah's youngest son (Genesis 5:32).
"Extender" (Hebrew)

Praise the LORD, for he has shown me his unfailing love. He kept me safe when my city was under attack. PSALM 31:21

Jehu JEE HYOO
There are two Jehus in the Old Testament: (1) The prophet who pronounced judgment upon Baasha and rebuked Jehoshaphat (1 Kings 16:1-7; 2 Chronicles 19:1-3); (2) The king of Northern Israel who had Jezebel and all the priests of Baal killed but continued to worship golden calves (2 Kings 9–10).
"God is He" (Hebrew)

"See, God has come to save me. I will trust in him and not be afraid. The LORD GOD is my strength and my song; he has become my salvation." ISAIAH 12:2

Jeremiah JERIH MIGH UH
He was known as the weeping prophet and authored the longest book in the Bible apart from Psalms (Jeremiah).
"Jehovah is high" (Hebrew)

What are mortals that you should think of us, mere humans that you should care for us? You put us in charge of everything you made, giving us authority over all things. PSALM 8:4, 6

Jeshua
Israel's first high priest after the return to rebuild Jerusalem (Zechariah 6:9-15).
"Jehovah saves" (Hebrew)

O LORD, I have longed for your salvation, and your law is my delight. PSALM 119:174

Jesse / *Jesse*

Sheepherder who was David's father (1 Samuel 16).
"God exists" (Hebrew)

Praise the LORD, for he has shown me his unfailing love.
He kept me safe when my city was under attack. PSALM 31:21

Jethro JETH ROH

Priest of Midian who became Moses' father-in-law (Exodus 3:1).
"Preeminence" (Hebrew)

The LORD lives! Blessed be my rock! May the God of my salvation be exalted! PSALM 18:46

Job JOHB

Hero of the book of Job.
"The persecuted" (Hebrew)

Be on guard. Stand true to what you believe. Be courageous.
Be strong. 1 CORINTHIANS 16:13

Jochebed JAHK UH BED

Moses' mother, a woman of faith, who hid baby Moses in a basket (Exodus 2).
"God is honor" (Hebrew)

The LORD is wonderfully good to those who wait for him and seek him. LAMENTATIONS 3:25

Joel

There are two Joels in the Old Testament: (1) The older of Samuel's two wicked sons (1 Samuel 8:2); and (2) Prophet who used a locust plague in his day to illustrate the coming great Tribulation (Joel).

"Jehovah is God" (Hebrew)

In the same way, let your good deeds shine out for all to see, so that everyone will praise your heavenly Father. MATTHEW 5:16

Johanan / *Johanan* JOH HAY NUHN

He forced Jeremiah to accompany him and a Jewish group to Egypt (Jeremiah 40–43).

"God is gracious" (Hebrew)

But the LORD still waits for you to come to him so he can show you his love and compassion. For the LORD is a faithful God. Blessed are those who wait for him to help them.

ISAIAH 30:18

Jonah JOH NUH

He survived being swallowed by a fish, and he preached in Nineveh (Jonah 2:10–3:5).

"Dove" (Hebrew), signifying peace

The LORD is my shepherd; I have everything I need. He lets me rest in green meadows; he leads me beside peaceful streams.

PSALM 23:1-2

Jonathan

There are two Jonathans in the Old Testament: (1) Saul's son and David's closest friend (1 Samuel 14:1; 18:1-4); (2) Son of

a chief priest, who undertook a dangerous mission to warn
David (2 Samuel 17:17-21).
"God has given" (Hebrew)

May the LORD smile on you and be gracious to you.
NUMBERS 6:25

Joseph
He was Jacob's favorite son, who used his position in Egypt to
rescue his family from famine (Genesis 37:3; 45:7-11).
"Increaser" (Hebrew)

*The wise are known for their understanding, and instruction is
appreciated if it's well presented.* PROVERBS 16:21

Joshua
Moses' successor, who led Israel into the Promised Land
(Joshua 1:1-3).
"Jehovah saves" (Hebrew)

*O LORD, I have longed for your salvation, and your law is my
delight.* PSALM 119:174

Josiah JOH SIGH UH
He was the last good king of Judah (2 Chronicles 34:2).
"God supports" (Hebrew)

*With all my heart I want your blessings. Be merciful just as you
promised.* PSALM 119:58

Jotham JOH THUHM
King of Judah who rebuilt the upper gate of the temple
(2 Chronicles 27:3).
"God is perfect" (Hebrew)

But the wisdom that comes from heaven is first of all pure. It is also peace loving, gentle at all times, and willing to yield to others. It is full of mercy and good deeds. It shows no partiality and is always sincere. JAMES 3:17

Judah JEW DUH

He was Jacob's fourth son, from whose line Christ would eventually come (Genesis 49:10; Hebrews 7:14).

"Praised" (Hebrew)

The LORD is wonderfully good to those who wait for him and seek him. LAMENTATIONS 3:25

Judith JEW DITH

A Hittite wife of Esau (Genesis 26:34) and the heroine of the apocryphal book of Judith.

"The praised." Feminine of Hebrew word for Judaean or Jew.

The LORD is wonderfully good to those who wait for him and seek him. LAMENTATIONS 3:25

Keturah KEH TYOO RUH

She was Abraham's third and final wife (Genesis 16:1-3; 25:1-8).

"Fragrance" (Hebrew)

I will offer you a sacrifice of thanksgiving and call on the name of the LORD. PSALM 116:17

Lamech LAY MEK

Prophet and Noah's father (Genesis 5:25-31).

"Overthrower" (Hebrew)

Learn to do good. Seek justice. Help the oppressed. Defend the orphan. Fight for the rights of widows. ISAIAH 1:17

Leah LEE UH

She bore Jacob six sons and one daughter (Genesis 29–30).
"Weary" (Hebrew)

But as for me, how good it is to be near God! I have made the Sovereign LORD my shelter, and I will tell everyone about the wonderful things you do. PSALM 73:28

Levi LEE VIGH

He was Jacob's third son, from whom the priestly line would come (Numbers 18:1-6).
"Joined" (Hebrew)

Do what is good and run from evil—that you may live! Then the LORD God Almighty will truly be your helper, just as you have claimed he is. AMOS 5:14

Mahlah MA LUH (A AS IN CAT)

She and her sisters requested and received from Moses the land rights of their father (Numbers 27:1-11).
"Mildness" (Hebrew)

The Sovereign LORD, the Holy One of Israel, says, "Only in returning to me and waiting for me will you be saved. In quietness and confidence is your strength." ISAIAH 30:15a

Malachi MAL UH KIGH

Prophet who wrote the final book of the Old Testament (Malachi).
"Messenger of God" (Hebrew)

I will sing of the tender mercies of the LORD forever! Young and old will hear of your faithfulness. PSALM 89:1

Micah / *Micah* MIGH KUH
There are two Micahs in the Old Testament: (1) Dishonest man who stole money from his mother and made an idol (Judges 17:1-11); and (2) Prophet who predicted that the birthplace of the Messiah would be Bethlehem (Micah 5:2; Matthew 2:6).
"Who is like God?" (Hebrew)

Spend your time and energy in training yourself for spiritual fitness. Physical exercise has some value, but spiritual exercise is much more important, for it promises a reward in both this life and the next. 1 TIMOTHY 4:7b-8

Micaiah / *Micaiah* MIGH KAY YUH
Godly and faithful prophet who was imprisoned by King Ahab (1 Kings 22:19-27).
"Who is like God?" (Hebrew)

Spend your time and energy in training yourself for spiritual fitness. Physical exercise has some value, but spiritual exercise is much more important, for it promises a reward in both this life and the next. 1 TIMOTHY 4:7b-8

Michael / *Michael*
The name of eleven Bible characters and the angel Michael, who appears in the books of Daniel, Jude, and Revelation.
"Who is like God?" (Hebrew)

Spend your time and energy in training yourself for spiritual fitness. Physical exercise has some value, but spiritual exercise is much more important, for it promises a reward in both this life and the next. 1 TIMOTHY 4:7b-8

Michal MIGH KUHL

She was Saul's youngest daughter and David's first wife (1 Samuel 14:49; 18:27).
"Who is like God?" (Hebrew)

Spend your time and energy in training yourself for spiritual fitness. Physical exercise has some value, but spiritual exercise is much more important, for it promises a reward in both this life and the next. 1 TIMOTHY 4:7b-8

Midian MID EE UHN

He was Abraham's son through Keturah and founded the Midianite people (Genesis 25:1-4).
"Contention" (Hebrew)

The LORD is good. When trouble comes, he is a strong refuge. And he knows everyone who trusts in him. NAHUM 1:7

Milcah MIL KUH

There are two Milcahs in the Old Testament: (1) The daughter of Haran, whose granddaughter was Rebekah (Genesis 24:15); and (2) One of the five daughters of Zelophehad of the tribe of Manasseh. Because they had no brothers, they were given an inheritance when the land was divided (Numbers 26:33).
"Counsel" (Hebrew)

For the LORD grants wisdom! From his mouth come knowledge and understanding. PROVERBS 2:6

Miriam MIHR EE UHM

She was Moses' only sister, who watched baby Moses in the

basket, and the first prophetess recorded in Scripture (Exodus 2, 15).

A Hebrew form of the name Mary, which means "bitter."

I will offer you a sacrifice of thanksgiving and call on the name of the LORD. PSALM 116:17

Moses

He was Israel's great lawgiver and author of the Pentateuch (Exodus 17:14; 24:5-7; Numbers 33:2; Deuteronomy 31:9; Joshua 23:6; Luke 24:27, 44; John 1:17; 5:46).

"The one drawn out" (Hebrew)

But giving thanks is a sacrifice that truly honors me. If you keep to my path, I will reveal to you the salvation of God.
PSALM 50:23

Naamah NAY UH MUH

There are two Naamahs in the Old Testament: (1) Daughter of Zillah and sister of Tubal-cain (Genesis 4:22); and (2) "The Ammonitess," the mother of Rehoboam (1 Kings 14:21).

"Pleasant" (Hebrew)

Kind words are like honey—sweet to the soul and healthy for the body. PROVERBS 16:24

Naaman NAY UH MUHN OR NAY MUHN

Cured of leprosy by Elisha (2 Kings 5:14).

"Pleasant" (Hebrew)

Kind words are like honey—sweet to the soul and healthy for the body. PROVERBS 16:24

Naomi NAY OH MEE
She was Ruth's mother-in-law (Ruth 1:3-6).
"Pleasant" (Hebrew)

Kind words are like honey—sweet to the soul
and healthy for the body. PROVERBS 16:24

Nathan NAY THUHN
There are two Nathans in the Old
Testament: (1) The prophet who
condemned David for the twin sins of
adultery and murder (2 Samuel 12:1-12);
and (2) He was one of David's sons by
Bathsheba, from whose line Mary was
born (1 Chronicles 3:4-5; Luke 3:31).
"Gift of the Lord" (Hebrew)

"But you are my witnesses, O Israel!" says the
LORD. "And you are my servant. You have
been chosen to know me, believe in me, and
understand that I alone am God. There is no
other God; there never has been and never
will be. ISAIAH 43:10

Nehemiah NEEHUH MIGH UH
He led the final Jewish return from Persia to Jerusalem and
rebuilt the wall around the city (Neh. 7:1).
"Jehovah is great" (Hebrew)

The LORD lives! Blessed be my rock! May the
God of my salvation be exalted! PSALM 18:46

---

*W*hy do you like
your name?

My full name is
Rebekah Elizabeth—a
different spelling than
the contemporary
Rebecca. I have found
the spelling of my
name to be a good
tool for witness. When
people notice that my
name is spelled
"differently," I take
the opportunity to tell
them that the spelling
is taken from the Old
Testament. Sometimes
then people will ask
me why, or what it
means. I've had some
pretty good conversa-
tions as a result.
Rebekah

Noah

He built an ark and survived the flood (Genesis 6–8).
"Peace" (Hebrew)

The LORD is my shepherd; I have everything I need. He lets me rest in green meadows; he leads me beside peaceful streams.
PSALM 23:1-2

Rachel

She was the beloved wife of Jacob and mother of both Joseph and Benjamin (Genesis 29:18; 30:23-24; 35:16-20).
"Lamb" (Hebrew), signifying gentle innocence

He will feed his flock like a shepherd. He will carry the lambs in his arms, holding them close to his heart. He will gently lead the mother sheep with their young. ISAIAH 40:11

Rebekah

She was Isaac's wife and Jacob's mother (Genesis 24:67; 25:26).
"The ensnarer" (Hebrew), signifying either a snare or a firm binding, like the marriage troth

But as for me, how good it is to be near God! I have made the Sovereign LORD my shelter, and I will tell everyone about the wonderful things you do. PSALM 73:28

Reuben

He was Jacob's first son (Genesis 49:1-3).
"Behold, a son" (Hebrew)

"So if the Son sets you free, you will indeed be free." JOHN 8:36

Ruth
A godly widow who became Boaz's wife and David's great-grandmother (Ruth).
"Friendship" (Hebrew)

There are "friends" who destroy each other, but a real friend sticks closer than a brother. PROVERBS 18:24

Samuel
Prophet and priest who anointed both Saul and David as king over Israel (1 Samuel 10:1, 2; 1 Samuel 16:1).
"Hand of God" (Hebrew)

The LORD is more pleased when we do what is just and right than when we give him sacrifices. PROVERBS 21:3

Sarah
She was Abraham's wife and Isaac's mother (Genesis 11:29; 21:1-7).
"Princess" (Hebrew)

But you are not like that, for you are a chosen people. You are a kingdom of priests, God's holy nation, his very own possession. This is so you can show others the goodness of God, for he called you out of the darkness into his wonderful light. 1 PETER 2:9

Sarai SEHR IGH (EYE)
Sarah's name before it was changed by God (Genesis 17:15).
Meaning unknown

But you are not like that, for you are a chosen people. You are a kingdom of priests, God's holy nation, his very own possession. This is so you can show others the goodness of God, for he called you out of the darkness into his wonderful light. 1 PETER 2:9

Saul

He was Israel's first king (1 Samuel 8–10).
"Asked for" (Hebrew)

To you, O LORD, I lift up my soul. I trust in you, my God! Do not let me be disgraced, or let my enemies rejoice in my defeat.
PSALM 25:1-2

Seraiah / *Seraiah* SIH RIGH UH OR SIH RAY YUH

There are two Seraiahs in the Old Testament: (1) Israel's final high priest before the Babylonian captivity (2 Kings 25:18-21); and (2) The brother of Baruch, Jeremiah's scribe, who carried a prophetic message for Jeremiah to Babylon (Jeremiah 32:12; 51:59-64).
"Warrior of God" (Hebrew)

Give honor to the LORD, you angels; give honor to the LORD for his glory and strength. PSALM 29:1

Seth

He was Adam's third son, whose line led to Christ (Genesis 4:1-2, 25; Luke 3:38).
"Compensation, sprout" (Hebrew)

The LORD will guide you continually, watering your life when you are dry and keeping you healthy, too. You will be like a well-watered garden, like an ever-flowing spring. ISAIAH 58:11

Shem

He was one of Noah's three sons from whose line the Jewish people came (1 Chronicles 1:24-27).
"Compensation, sprout" (Hebrew)

The LORD will guide you continually, watering your life when

you are dry and keeping you healthy, too. You will be like a
well-watered garden, like an ever-flowing spring.
ISAIAH 58:11

Sherah SHEE RUH
Daughter of Ephraim. She built the city of Beth-horon
(1 Chronicles 7:24).
"A female relative" (Hebrew)

But you are not like that, for you are a chosen people. You are a
kingdom of priests, God's holy nation, his very own possession.
This is so you can show others the goodness of God, for he called
you out of the darkness into his wonderful light. 1 PETER 2:9

Shua SHOO UH
Daughter of Heber of the tribe of Asher (1 Chronicles 7:32).
Hebrew name of unknown origin

Lead me in the right path, O LORD, or my enemies will conquer
me. PSALM 5:8

Simeon SIM EE UHN
He was Jacob's second son, and his line became one of the
twelve tribes of Israel (Genesis 29:33).
"Hearing" (Hebrew)

Commit everything you do to the LORD. Trust him, and he will
help you. PSALM 37:5

Solomon SAHL UH MUHN
He was the world's wisest man (1 Kings 3:11-12).
"Peace" (Hebrew)

The LORD is my shepherd; I have everything I need. He lets me rest in green meadows; he leads me beside peaceful streams.
PSALM 23:1-2

Tamar TAY MAHR

There are two Tamars in the Old Testament: (1) Judah's daughter-in-law, who bore him twins and became an ancestress to David and Christ (Genesis 38:12-30; Matthew 1:3); and (2) David's daughter, who was raped by her half-brother Amnon (2 Samuel 13:1-19).

"Palm" (Hebrew), signifying the beauty and fruitfulness of the tree.

The LORD will guide you continually, watering your life when you are dry and keeping you healthy, too. You will be like a well-watered garden, like an ever-flowing spring. ISAIAH 58:11

Terah / *Terah* TEE RUH OR TEHR UH

He was the father of Abraham and Sarah (Genesis 11:26; 20:12).

"Turning, duration" (Hebrew)

And I am sure that God, who began the good work within you, will continue his work until it is finally finished on that day when Christ Jesus comes back again. PHILIPPIANS 1:6

Vashti VASH TEE

She was a queen who refused to display and parade herself before her husband's drunken friends, and so her husband, King Ahasuerus, divorced her (Esther 1).

"Beautiful" (Persian)

Since we are receiving a kingdom that cannot be destroyed, let us be thankful and please God by worshiping him with holy fear and awe. HEBREWS 12:28

Zebadiah ZEB UH DIGH UH

Zebadiah is the name of several minor Old Testament characters, including the Temple doorkeeper (1 Chronicles 26:2) and an officer of David (1 Chronicles 27:7).
"Gift of the Lord" (Hebrew)

May the LORD smile on you and be gracious to you.
NUMBERS 6:25

Zechariah ZEK UH RIGH UH

There are two Zechariahs in the Old Testament: (1) The fearless high priest in the days of King Joash (2 Chronicles 24:20-22); and (2) A prophet whose book, for its size, has more to say about both Christ's first and second coming than any other Old Testament book (Zechariah).
"God has remembered" (Hebrew)

Show me your unfailing love in wonderful ways. You save with your strength those who seek refuge from their enemies.
PSALM 17:7

Zephaniah ZEF UH NIGH UH

He used the term "the Day of the Lord" more often than any other Old Testament prophet (Zephaniah).
"He whom God hath hidden" (Hebrew)

You would not be pleased with sacrifices, or I would bring them. If I brought you a burnt offering, you would not accept it.
PSALM 51:16

Zipporah ZI POH RUH

She was Moses' wife (Exodus 2:21).
"Little bird" (Hebrew)

I will delight in your principles and not forget your word.

PSALM 119:16

New Testament Names

*W*hether you're looking for a common name (Mary, John) or something a little bit offbeat (Jairus, Magdalene), the New Testament provides an excellent variety of name choices. Whatever your choice, these names will give your child a sense of connection to the time of the New Testament.

Alexander

There are five Alexanders in the New Testament: (1) The son of Simon of Cyrene; (2) A member of the high-priestly family, unknown apart from Acts 4:6; (3) The would-be spokesman of the Jewish interest in the Ephesian riot (Acts 19:33); (4) A corrupt teacher (1 Timothy 1:20); and (5) An enemy of Paul (2 Timothy 4:14).
"Protecting men" (Greek)

So be strong and take courage, all you who put your hope in the LORD! PSALM 31:24

Andrew

One of the twelve disciples, he brought his brother Peter to Christ (John 1:40-42).
"Strong, manly" (Greek)

"I thank and praise you, God of my ancestors, for you have given me wisdom and strength. You have told me what we asked of you and revealed to us what the king demanded."

DANIEL 2:23

Anna

Prophetess who gave thanks to God at the dedication of the infant Jesus (Luke 2:36-38).
"Graceful one" (Hebrew)

I am determined to keep your principles, even forever, to the very end. PSALM 119:112

Apphia AF EE UH
Probably the wife of Philemon (Philemon 2).
Meaning unknown, probably native Phrygian

I am praying to you because I know you will answer, O God. Bend down and listen as I pray. PSALM 17:6

Barnabas
Preacher who accompanied Paul on his first missionary journey (Acts 15).
"Son of encouragement" (Hebrew)

Reverence for the LORD is the foundation of true wisdom. The rewards of wisdom come to all who obey him. Praise his name forever! PSALM 111:10

Bartholomew
Also known as Nathanael. Philip witnessed to him under a fig tree and brought him to Christ. He became one of the twelve disciples (John 1:45-51).
"Gift of God" (Hebrew)

May the LORD smile on you and be gracious to you.
NUMBERS 6:25

Bartimaeus BAHR TIH MAY UHS
He received his sight at the hand of Jesus (Mark 10:46-52).
"Son of Timaeus"

But God is my helper. The Lord is the one who keeps me alive!
PSALM 54:4

Bernice

She was a queen who heard the imprisoned Paul preach in
Caesarea (Acts 25–26).
"Harbinger of victory" (Greek)

*The LORD, your Redeemer, the Holy One of Israel, says: I am
the LORD your God, who teaches you what is good and leads you
along the paths you should follow.* ISAIAH 48:17

Candace

Ethiopian queen whose minister was converted under the
ministry of Philip (Acts 8:27-38).
"Glittering, glowing white" (Greek)

*The Sovereign LORD is my strength! He will make me as
surefooted as a deer and bring me safely over the mountains.*
HABAKKUK 3:19

Clement

Philippian Christian and friend of Paul (Philippians 4:3).
"Kind, gentle, mild, merciful" (Latin)

*Lead me in the right path, O LORD, or my enemies will conquer
me.* PSALM 5:8

Cleopas KLEE OH PUHS

He was joined by the resurrected Christ on the first Easter
Sunday en route to Emmaus (Luke 24:18).
Meaning unknown

If you look for me in earnest, you will find me when you seek me.
JEREMIAH 29:13

Cornelius
He sent for and was led to Christ by the apostle Peter at Caesarea, becoming the first Gentile convert to Christianity (Acts 10).
"A horn" (Latin), suggesting a vigilant spirit

Be glad for all God is planning for you. Be patient in trouble, and always be prayerful. ROMANS 12:12

Crispus / *Crispus* KRISS PUHS
He was Paul's first recorded convert in Corinth (Acts 18:8).
"Curled" (Latin)

The LORD is wonderfully good to those who wait for him and seek him. LAMENTATIONS 3:25

Demas DEE MUHS
A coworker with Paul during his first imprisonment (Philemon 1:24; Colossians 4:14).
Meaning unknown

Give honor to the LORD, you angels; give honor to the LORD for his glory and strength. PSALM 29:1

Dorcas DAWR KUHS
Also known as Tabitha, she was raised from the dead by Peter at Joppa (Acts 9).
"Gazelle, roe" (Greek)

As the deer pants for streams of water, so I long for you, O God.
PSALM 42:1

Elizabeth

She miraculously gave birth to John (the Baptist) in her old age (Luke 1).
"God's oath" (Hebrew)

Give me understanding and I will obey your law; I will put it into practice with all my heart. PSALM 119:34

Emmanuel / *Emmanuelle* IH MAN YOO EL

Another name for Jesus Christ (Matthew 1:23).
"God with us" (Hebrew)

For I can do everything with the help of Christ who gives me the strength I need. PHILIPPIANS 4:13

Eunice

She was the godly mother of Timothy (Acts 16:1; 2 Timothy 1:5).
"Happily victorious" (Greek)

Sing about the glory of his name! Tell the world how glorious he is. PSALM 66:2

Jairus JIGH RUHS OR JAY UH RUHS

Jesus raised his daughter from the dead (Mark 5:22-43).
"Enlightened by God" (Hebrew)

What are mortals that you should think of us, mere humans that you should care for us? You put us in charge of everything you made, giving us authority over all things. PSALM 8:4, 6

James

There are three Jameses in the New Testament: (1) A fisherman and brother of John who became one of Christ's

three key apostles (Matthew 4:21-22; 17:1; Mark 14:33);
(2) A brother of Christ who pastored the church at Jerusalem
and authored the New Testament book of James (John 7:3-5;
Acts 15:13-14, 19; James); and (3) James the Less, who was
one of the twelve apostles.
"Supplanter," a form of Jacob. The Lord molded Jacob into a
man after God's heart.

*Those who lead blameless lives and do what is right, speaking the
truth from sincere hearts. Those who do not charge interest on the
money they lend, and who refuse to accept bribes to testify against
the innocent. Such people will stand firm forever.*
PSALM 15:2, 5

Jason
He was a convert of Paul, living in Thessalonica, whom the
Jews persecuted (Acts 17:5-9).
"Healing" (Greek)

*The Spirit of the Sovereign LORD is upon me, because the LORD
has appointed me to bring good news to the poor. He has sent me
to comfort the brokenhearted and to announce that captives will
be released and prisoners will be freed.* ISAIAH 61:1

Joanna
She helped Jesus financially in Galilee and was one of the
women visiting the tomb of Christ on Sunday to finish his
burial preparation (Luke 8:1-3).
"God is Gracious" (Hebrew)

*But the LORD still waits for you to come to him so he can show
you his love and compassion. For the LORD is a faithful God.
Blessed are those who wait for him to help them.* ISAIAH 30:18

John

There are two Johns in the New Testament: (1) Christ's
beloved disciple who authored five New Testament books;
and (2) John the Baptist, the forerunner of Christ; he both
introduced and baptized the Messiah (John 1:15-27).
"The grace of Jehovah" (Hebrew)

May the LORD smile on you and be gracious to you.

NUMBERS 6:25

John Mark

Author and missionary evangelist who wrote the Gospel of
Mark (Acts 12:25).
John "Grace of Jehovah" (Hebrew); Mark "Warlike one"
(Latin)

*Give honor to the LORD, you angels; give honor to the LORD for
his glory and strength.* PSALM 29:1

Joseph

There are two Josephs in the New Testament: (1) The godly
legal (but not physical) father of Jesus (Matthew 1:18-24);
and (2) A wealthy man from Arimathea who obtained the
lifeless body of Jesus from the cross and placed it in the
tomb he had purchased for himself (Mark 15:44-46).
"Increaser, may God add" (Hebrew)

*The wise are known for their understanding, and instruction is
appreciated if it's well presented.* PROVERBS 16:21

Jude / *Jude*

He was the half brother of Christ and the author of the New
Testament book of Jude (Acts 15:22-23).

"Praised" (Hebrew). A form of Judas or Judah.

The LORD is wonderfully good to those who wait for him and seek him. LAMENTATIONS 3:25

Julia

Friend of Paul (Romans 16:15).
"Youthful one" (Latin)

O Lord, you alone are my hope. I've trusted you, O LORD, from childhood. PSALM 71:5

Julius

He commanded the ship that carried Paul to Rome (Acts 27).
"Descended from Jove (Jupiter)" (Latin)

I long to obey your commandments! Renew my life with your goodness. PSALM 119:40

Linus

A Roman Christian who greeted Timothy (2 Timothy 4:21).
"Flaxen-colored" (Latin)

The one thing I ask of the LORD—the thing I seek most—is to live in the house of the LORD all the days of my life, delighting in the LORD's perfections and meditating in his Temple.
PSALM 27:4

Lois

Grandmother of Timothy (2 Timothy 1:5).
"Famous warrior-maid" (Hebrew)

How we thank God, who gives us victory over sin and death through Jesus Christ our Lord! 1 CORINTHIANS 15:57

Luke

He was the author of the books of Luke and
Acts and served as Paul's personal physician.
"Light giving" (Latin)

*You have heard me teach many things that
have been confirmed by many reliable
witnesses. Teach these great truths to trustworthy people who are able to pass them on
to others.* 2 TIMOTHY 2:2

Lydia

She was Paul's first female convert in Greece
(Acts 16:14-15).
"From Lydia." A Greek place, *Lydios,* was an ancient part of
Asia Minor known for its fine culture.

*I am praying to you because I know you will answer, O God.
Bend down and listen as I pray.* PSALM 17:6

Magdalene

Mary Magdalene was a woman who had been
demon-possessed but became a believer and was the first
person to see the resurrected Christ (Mark 16:9; John 20).
"A tower" (Hebrew)

*But as for me, I will sing about your power. I will shout with
joy each morning because of your unfailing love. For you have
been my refuge, a place of safety in the day of distress.*
PSALM 59:16

Why do you like your name?

The Mark in the
Bible is an interest-
ing character—he's
not perfect, but he
comes through in
the end. It's fun to
have a name that's
connected with
the Bible.
Mark

Mark

Author and missionary who wrote the Gospel of Mark. Also known as John Mark (Acts 12:25).
"Warlike one" (Latin)

Give honor to the LORD, you angels; give honor to the LORD for his glory and strength. PSALM 29:1

Martha

She saw Christ raise her dead brother, Lazarus (John 11).
"Lady, mistress"(Aramean)

Fear of the LORD teaches a person to be wise; humility precedes honor. PROVERBS 15:33

Mary

There are four Marys in the New Testament: (1) Mary the mother of Jesus, God's chosen vessel to give birth to the Savior of the world (Luke 1, 2); (2) Mary Magdalene, the first person to see the resurrected Christ (John 20); (3) Mary, the mother of James and Joseph, who helped Christ financially and was present at his crucifixion and resurrection (Mark 15:40); and (4) Mary, the sister of Martha, who anointed Christ with precious oil (John 12:1-3).
"Bitter" (Hebrew)

I will offer you a sacrifice of thanksgiving and call on the name of the LORD. PSALM 116:17

Matthew

Tax collector who became an apostle and author of the Gospel of Matthew (Luke 5:27-29).
"Gift of God" (Hebrew)

May the LORD smile on you and be gracious to you. NUMBERS 6:25

Matthias
He was selected to take the place of Judas Iscariot (Acts 1:23-26).
"Gift of Jehovah" (Hebrew)
May the LORD smile on you and be gracious to you. NUMBERS 6:25

Nathanael
Also known as Bartholomew. Philip witnessed to him under a fig tree and brought him to Christ. He became one of the twelve disciples (John 1:45-51).
"Gift of God" (Hebrew)

"But you are my witnesses, O Israel!" says the LORD. "And you are my servant. You have been chosen to know me, believe in me, and understand that I alone am God. There is no other God; there never has been and never will be." ISAIAH 43:10

Nicodemus NIK UH DEE MUHS
He was a Jewish religious leader who came to Christ by night, asking about the new birth (John 3).
"Victor over the people"(Greek)

The LORD lives! Blessed be my rock! May the God of my salvation be exalted! PSALM 18:46

Paul
Born Saul. He was the greatest missionary, church planter, soul winner, and theologian in church history. He wrote

Why do you like your name?
I didn't like my name at first because it means "small," but when I realized the importance of the role Paul the apostle played in the church, I took pride in the fact that I was named after someone who was used by God in such a great way in spreading the gospel.
Paul

thirteen (perhaps fourteen) of the twenty-seven New Testament books.
"Little, small" (Latin), signifying dependence on God

But as for me, how good it is to be near God! I have made the Sovereign LORD my shelter, and I will tell everyone about the wonderful things you do. PSALM 73:28

Peter

He was one of the chief apostles and author of two New Testament books (1 Peter; 2 Peter).
"Rock" (Greek)

Wait patiently for the LORD. Be brave and courageous. Yes, wait patiently for the LORD. PSALM 27:14

Philip

There are two Philips in the New Testament: (1) The apostle who led Nathanael to Christ (John 1:45-46); and (2) A believer who led the Ethiopian eunuch to Christ in the desert of Gaza (Acts 8:26-40).
"Lover of horses" (Greek)

He will give you all you need from day to day if you live for him and make the Kingdom of God your primary concern.
MATTHEW 6:33

Phoebe FEE BEE

She was a deaconess and carried Paul's Epistle to the Romans to the church at Rome (Romans 16:1).
"Bright, radiant" (Greek)

You have heard me teach many things that have been confirmed by many reliable witnesses. Teach these great truths to trustworthy people who are able to pass them on to others. 2 TIMOTHY 2:2

Priscilla / Prisca
She and her husband greatly assisted and encouraged the apostle Paul (Acts 18).
"Ancient" (Latin). A name derived from the title of a Latin clan, so called for its great antiquity

As for me, I look to the LORD for his help. I wait confidently for God to save me, and my God will certainly hear me.
MICAH 7:7

Rhoda
She reported the release of Simon Peter from prison (Acts 12:14).
"A rose" (Greek)

I will sacrifice a voluntary offering to you; I will praise your name, O LORD, for it is good. PSALM 54:6

Rufus
Friend of Paul who lived in Rome (Romans 16:13).
"Redhead" (Latin)

Give honor to the LORD, you angels; give honor to the LORD for his glory and strength. PSALM 29:1

Silas
He was Paul's faithful associate during his second missionary journey (Acts 15–16).
"Asked of God" (Hebrew?)

*He will give you all you need from day to day if you live for him
and make the Kingdom of God your primary concern.*
MATTHEW 6:33

Simeon SIM EE UHN
He blessed the infant Jesus in the Jerusalem temple (Luke
2:25-34).
"Hearing" (Hebrew)

*Commit everything you do to the LORD. Trust him, and he will
help you.* PSALM 37:5

Simon SIGH MUHN
There are six Simons in the New Testament: (1) Simon the
Cyrenian, who carried Jesus' cross to Calvary (Matthew
27:32); (2) Simon the leper, who hosted a supper to celebrate
the raising of Lazarus (Matthew 26:6); (3) Simon the
Pharisee, whom Jesus ate supper with but had to rebuke for
the sin of hypocrisy (Luke 7:40-44); (4) Simon the sorcerer,
whom Peter severely rebuked for attempting to buy the
power of the Holy Spirit (Acts 8:9-24); (5) Simon Peter (see
Peter); and (6) Simon the Zealot, the political conservative
among Christ's twelve disciples (Matthew 10:4).
"Hearing" (Hebrew)

*Commit everything you do to the LORD. Trust him, and he will
help you.* PSALM 37:5

Stephanas / *Stephanas*
He was Paul's first male convert in Greece (1 Corinthians 1:16).
"Crown" (Greek)

Praise the LORD, I tell myself, and never forget the good things he does for me. He ransoms me from death and surrounds me with love and tender mercies. PSALM 103:2, 4

Stephen STEE VUHN
He was the first recorded martyr in the early church (Acts 7:54-60).
"Crown, wreath" (Greek)
Praise the LORD, I tell myself, and never forget the good things he does for me. He ransoms me from death and surrounds me with love and tender mercies. PSALM 103:2, 4

Syntyche SIN TIH KEE
This godly helper of Paul had experienced a falling out with another woman in the church at Philippi (Philippians 4:2).
"Fortunate"
Such people will not be overcome by evil circumstances. Those who are righteous will be long remembered. PSALM 112:6

Tabitha TAB IH THUH
She (who was also called Dorcas) was raised from the dead by Peter at Joppa (Acts 9).
"Gazelle" (Aramaic)
As the deer pants for streams of water, so I long for you, O God. PSALM 42:1

Thaddaeus THAD EE UHS
Also known as "Judas of James," he was the last of the three disciples who asked Jesus a question during the final Passover in the upper room (John 14:22-23).
"The praised" (Hebrew)

For I can do everything with the help of Christ who gives me the strength I need. PHILIPPIANS 4:13

Thomas

The disciple who asked for proof that Jesus had indeed been raised from the dead (John 20:24-25).
"Twin" (Hebrew)

O God, you are my God; I earnestly search for you. My soul thirsts for you; my whole body longs for you in this parched and weary land where there is no water. PSALM 63:1

Timothy

Missionary and pastor; Paul addressed two New Testament epistles to him (1, 2 Timothy).
"Honored of God" (Greek)

Praise the LORD, I tell myself; O LORD my God, how great you are! You are robed with honor and with majesty. PSALM 104:1

Titus TIGH TUHS

Missionary and pastor; Paul addressed a New Testament epistle to him (Titus).
"The safe, or saved" (Latin) or "giant" (Greek)

O LORD, I have longed for your salvation, and your law is my delight. PSALM 119:174

Tryphena TRIGH FEE NUH

Friend of Paul (Romans 16:12).
Meaning unknown

There are "friends" who destroy each other, but a real friend sticks closer than a brother. PROVERBS 18:24

Tryphosa TRIGH FOH SUH
Friend of Paul (Romans 16:12).
Meaning unknown

There are "friends" who destroy each other, but a real friend sticks closer than a brother. PROVERBS 18:24

Zacchaeus ZA KEE UHS
This dishonest tax collector met Jesus while in a sycamore tree and later became a believer in Christ (Luke 19:1-9).
"Pure"

"I take joy in doing your will, my God, for your law is written on my heart." PSALM 40:8

Zechariah ZEK UH RIGH UH
Father of John the Baptist (Luke 1).
"God remembers" (Hebrew)

Show me your unfailing love in wonderful ways. You save with your strength those who seek refuge from their enemies.
PSALM 17:7

Place-Names

*U*sing place-names as personal names is common across America; names like Madison, Dakota, Denver, and Savannah are inching their way up the charts.
Bible places offer a wide variety of familiar (Bethany, Jordan) or distinctive (Arabah, Tyre) names. The names listed in this section reflect areas with a positive history. (Infamous places such as Babylon and Sodom have been left behind!) With your parental guidance, these place-names can become a meaningful anchor to the lands of the Bible.

Alexandria

The home of Apollos, a follower of Christ. The city was
named after Alexander the Great (Acts 18:24-26).
"Helper of mankind" (Greek)

*Live in such a way that God's love can bless you as you wait for
the eternal life that our Lord Jesus Christ in his mercy is going to
give you.* JUDE 1:21

Arabah (A) RUH BAH or AH RUH BAH

The rift valley that runs from the Sea of Gallilee to the Gulf
of Aqabah (Joshua 18:18).
"Wilderness, desert" (Hebrew)

*Praise the LORD! Give thanks to the LORD, for he is good! His
faithful love endures forever. Who can list the glorious miracles of
the LORD? Who can ever praise him half enough? He commanded
the Red Sea to divide, and a dry path appeared. He led Israel
across the sea bottom that was as dry as a desert.*

PSALM 106:1-2, 9

Arimathea AR IH MUH THEE UH

The home of Joseph, who, along with Nicodemus, claimed
the body of Jesus Christ (Matthew 27:57-60).
"A city of the Jews" (Hebrew)

And having chosen them, he called them to come to him. And he gave them right standing with himself, and he promised them his glory. ROMANS 8:30

Athens ATH IHNZ
The capital city of Greece, where Paul preached his Mars Hill sermon (Acts 17:15-34).
Meaning unknown

But the LORD still waits for you to come to him so he can show you his love and compassion. For the LORD is a faithful God. Blessed are those who wait for him to help them. ISAIAH 30:18

Berea BUH REE UH
A place of Scripture-loving Christians, who were visited by Paul on his first missionary journey (Acts 17:10-12).
Meaning unknown

I take joy in doing your will, my God, for your law is written on my heart. PSALM 40:8

Bethany BETH UH NEE
The city where Lazarus was raised from the dead, Mary anointed the feet of Jesus, and the Lord blessed his disciples right before his ascension (Luke 24:50; John 11; 12:1-11).
"Worshiper of God" or "house of poverty" (Aramaic)

I am praying to you because I know you will answer, O God. Bend down and listen as I pray. PSALM 17:6

Bethel BETH UHL
The place where Abraham worshiped God when he came to Palestine, and where Jacob dreamed his "ladder" dream. (Genesis 12:8; 13:3-4; 28:11-19)

"House of God" (Hebrew)

I am praying to you because I know you will answer, O God. Bend down and listen as I pray. PSALM 17:6

Bethesda BUH THEZ DUH

The name of a pool in Jerusalem, whose waters were believed to be healing. Jesus healed a man there (John 5:2-8).

"House of mercy" or "place of flowing water" (Hebrew)

"If you believe in me, come and drink! For the Scriptures declare that rivers of living water will flow out from within."

JOHN 7:38

Bethsaida BETH SAY IH DUH

Home of Philip, Andrew, and Peter, where Jesus healed a blind man (Mark 8:22-26; John 1:44).

"House of fishing" (Aramaic)

Jesus called out to them, "Come, be my disciples, and I will show you how to fish for people!" MARK 1:17

Cana KAY NUH

This town is best known as the place where Jesus performed his first miracle, that of turning water into wine (John 2:1-11; 4:46-54; 21:2).

"Place of reeds" (Hebrew)

The Spirit of the Sovereign LORD is upon me, because the LORD has appointed me to bring good news to the poor. He has sent me to comfort the brokenhearted and to announce that captives will be released and prisoners will be freed. ISAIAH 61:1

Carmel / *Carmela* KAHR M'L or KAHR M'L (A)
A mountain in Palestine famous for the deeds of the prophets Elijah and Elisha (Isaiah 16:10).
"Garden land" or "fruitful land" (Hebrew)

I long to obey your commandments! Renew my life with your goodness. PSALM 119:40

Cyrene SIGH REE NEE
A port in northern Africa that was the home of Simon, who carried Jesus' cross (Matthew 27:32).
Meaning unknown

O LORD, I have longed for your salvation, and your law is my delight. PSALM 119:174

Eden / Eden EE DUHN
The name of the garden that God made for Adam and Eve to live in and from which they were driven after the Fall (Genesis 2:8–3:24).
"Delightful, pleasant" (Hebrew)

Take delight in the LORD, and he will give you your heart's desires. PSALM 37:4

Israel IZ RAY EL
Nation descended from the twelve tribes (Genesis 34:7); also, the new name given to Jacob after his night of wrestling at Peniel (Genesis 32:22-28).
"God strives" (Hebrew)

With all my heart I want your blessings. Be merciful just as you promised. PSALM 119:58

Jordan / **Jordan** JAWR DUHN

The most significant river in the Bible; site of Christ's
baptism (Mark 1:9-11).

"The descender" (Hebrew). The Jordan River "descends" into
the Dead Sea.

*If you believe in me, come and drink! For the Scriptures declare
that rivers of living water will flow out from within.* JOHN 7:38

Lydda LID UH

The town where Peter cured Aeneas (Acts 9:32-35).

Meaning unknown

*The Spirit of the Sovereign LORD is upon me, because the LORD
has appointed me to bring good news to the poor. He has sent me
to comfort the brokenhearted and to announce that captives will
be released and prisoners will be freed.* ISAIAH 61:1

Lystra LISS TRUH

The home of Timothy, where Paul was stoned (Acts 14:19;
16:1-4; 2 Timothy 3:11).

Meaning unknown

*Be on guard. Stand true to what you believe. Be courageous.
Be strong.* 1 CORINTHIANS 16:13

Magdala MAG DUH LUH

A locale on the west side of the Sea of Galilee, and the home
of Mary Magdalene (Mark 16:9; Luke 8:2).

"A tower" (Hebrew)

*The LORD is my rock, my fortress, and my savior; my God is my
rock, in whom I find protection. He is my shield, the strength of
my salvation, and my stronghold.* PSALM 18:2

Marah MAH RUH

First camp of the Israelites after the Red Sea crossing; it was called Marah because only bitter water was found there.
"Bitter" (Hebrew)

Happy are those who obey his decrees and search for him with all their hearts. PSALM 119:2

Myra MIGH RUH

Located on the southwest tip of Asia Minor, Paul changed ships there as a prisoner en route to Rome (Acts 27:5-6).
"The wonderful" (Latin)

I will be filled with joy because of you. I will sing praises to your name, O Most High. PSALM 9:2

Nain NAYN

A small village where Jesus raised a widow's son from the dead (Luke 7:11-18).
"Pleasant" (Hebrew)

Kind words are like honey—sweet to the soul and healthy for the body. PROVERBS 16:24

Olivet AHL IH VET

Olivet (also called the Mount of Olives) is a small range of four summits which overlooks Jerusalem and where Jesus will return at his second coming (Zechariah 14:4).
"The olive tree" (Hebrew)

Oh, the joys of those who do not follow the advice of the wicked, or stand around with sinners, or join in with scoffers. They are like trees planted along the riverbank, bearing fruit each season without fail. Their leaves never wither, and in all they do, they prosper. PSALM 1:1, 3

Peraea PUH REE UH
A district in Transjordan where Jewish people lived in the time of Christ (Matthew 19:1).
Meaning unknown

See, God has come to save me. I will trust in him and not be afraid. The LORD GOD is my strength and my song; he has become my salvation. ISAIAH 12:2

Shiloh / *Shiloh* SHIGH LOH
The home of the tabernacle after Israel conquered Palestine, where Hannah prayed for a son, and where God called to young Samuel (Joshua 18:1; 1 Samuel 1; 3:21).
Possibly "tranquility" (Hebrew)

If you do this, you will experience God's peace, which is far more wonderful than the human mind can understand. His peace will guard your hearts and minds as you live in Christ Jesus.
PHILIPPIANS 4:7

Troas TROH AZ
The city where Paul received his Macedonian vision (Acts 16:11; 20:6-12; 2 Timothy 4:13).
Meaning unknown

But you are not like that, for you are a chosen people. You are a kingdom of priests, God's holy nation, his very own possession. This is so you can show others the goodness of God, for he called you out of the darkness into his wonderful light. 1 PETER 2:9

Tyre TIGHR
The seaport city of Ezekiel's great prophecy where Paul knelt down by the seashore and prayed (Ezekiel 26; Acts 21:2-6). "Rock" (Arabic)

Wait patiently for the LORD. Be brave and courageous. Yes, wait patiently for the LORD. PSALM 27:14

Precious Stone Names

Names like Ruby and Pearl have been around for generations, but did you ever realize that these jewels are mentioned in the Bible? Many of the precious stones listed below are found in the Lord's instructions for furnishing the temple, adorning the high priest's robes, and in the description of heaven.

The mention of these stones shows us that the Lord also thought these stones were of great beauty and value—just as your child is of great beauty and value in God's eyes!

Amethyst

A purple variety of precious stone. The February birthstone, it is one of the stones found in the high priest's breastplate (Exodus 28:19; Revelation 21:20).
"Wine-colored" (Greek)

When that day arrives, the LORD their God will rescue his people, just as a shepherd rescues his sheep. They will sparkle in his land like jewels in a crown. How wonderful and beautiful they will be! The young men and women will thrive on the abundance of grain and new wine. ZECHARIAH 9:16-17

Beryl

Probably Spanish gold topaz, known to the ancient world as chrysolite. One of the stones found in the high priest's breastplate (Exodus 28:20).
"Dazzling jewel" (Greek)

When that day arrives, the LORD their God will rescue his people, just as a shepherd rescues his sheep. They will sparkle in his land like jewels in a crown. How wonderful and beautiful they will be! The young men and women will thrive on the abundance of grain and new wine. ZECHARIAH 9:16-17

Coral

A red or black precious stone consisting of the skeletons of innumerable small marine polyps (Job 28:18; Ezekiel 27:16). "From the coral of the sea" (Greek)

When that day arrives, the LORD their God will rescue his people, just as a shepherd rescues his sheep. They will sparkle in his land like jewels in a crown. How wonderful and beautiful they will be! The young men and women will thrive on the abundance of grain and new wine. ZECHARIAH 9:16-17

Crystal

A translucent substance (Job 28:18). "Brilliantly pure" (Greek)

When that day arrives, the LORD their God will rescue his people, just as a shepherd rescues his sheep. They will sparkle in his land like jewels in a crown. How wonderful and beautiful they will be! The young men and women will thrive on the abundance of grain and new wine. ZECHARIAH 9:16-17

Jacinth JAY SINTH

A blue stone, such as turquoise. One of the stones found in the high priest's breastplate (Exodus 28:19; Revelation 21:20). Meaning unknown

When that day arrives, the LORD their God will rescue his people, just as a shepherd rescues his sheep. They will sparkle in his land like jewels in a crown. How wonderful and beautiful they will be! The young men and women will thrive on the abundance of grain and new wine. ZECHARIAH 9:16-17

Jasper / *Jasper*

A translucent green stone. One of the stones found in the
high priest's breastplate (Revelation 4:3; 21:11).
"The bearer of treasure" (Persian)

*When that day arrives, the LORD their God will rescue his
people, just as a shepherd rescues his sheep. They will sparkle in
his land like jewels in a crown. How wonderful and beautiful
they will be! The young men and women will thrive on the
abundance of grain and new wine.* ZECHARIAH 9:16-17

Pearl

The gates of the new Jerusalem will be made of this
(Revelation 21:21).
"A pearl" (Greek)

*The Kingdom of Heaven is like a pearl merchant on the lookout
for choice pearls. When he discovered a pearl of great value, he
sold everything he owned and bought it!* MATTHEW 13:45-46

Ruby

A red stone found in the high priest's breastplate (Exodus
28:17-20).
"Deep red" (Latin)

*When that day arrives, the LORD their God will rescue his
people, just as a shepherd rescues his sheep. They will sparkle in
his land like jewels in a crown. How wonderful and beautiful
they will be! The young men and women will thrive on the
abundance of grain and new wine.* ZECHARIAH 9:16-17

Sapphire

The ancient name for lapis lazuli, a deep blue stone with golden flecks; one of the stones found in the high priest's breastplate (Exodus 24:10).
"Precious gem" (Hebrew)

When that day arrives, the LORD their God will rescue his people, just as a shepherd rescues his sheep. They will sparkle in his land like jewels in a crown. How wonderful and beautiful they will be! The young men and women will thrive on the abundance of grain and new wine. ZECHARIAH 9:16-17

Topaz

A yellow stone found in the high priest's breastplate (Exodus 28:17).
Meaning unknown

When that day arrives, the LORD their God will rescue his people, just as a shepherd rescues his sheep. They will sparkle in his land like jewels in a crown. How wonderful and beautiful they will be! The young men and women will thrive on the abundance of grain and new wine. ZECHARIAH 9:16-17

Nature Names

*P*lant and flower names like Ivy, Rose, Fern, Pansy, and Dahlia have seen their day in American culture. Bible flower and tree names hold some interesting possibilities. Not only are these flowers and trees indigenous to the Promised Land, they also celebrate the beauty of God's creation.

Acacia UH KAY SHUH

Tree of which parts of the tabernacle were to be made
(Exodus 25).

*Oh, the joys of those who do not follow the advice of the wicked,
or stand around with sinners, or join in with scoffers. They are
like trees planted along the riverbank, bearing fruit each season
without fail. Their leaves never wither, and in all they do, they
prosper.* PSALM 1:1, 3

Cassia KASH UH

Plant that was made into a perfume (Exodus 30:24).

*But thanks be to God, who made us his captives and leads us
along in Christ's triumphal procession. Now wherever we go
he uses us to tell others about the Lord and to spread the Good
News like a sweet perfume.*

2 CORINTHIANS 2:14

Ebony

The reddish black heartwood of a tree that grows in Africa,
used extensively for fine furniture and carvings (Ezekiel
27:15).

*Happy is the person who finds wisdom and gains understanding.
For the profit of wisdom is better than silver, and her wages are*

better than gold. Wisdom is a tree of life to those who embrace her; happy are those who hold her tightly. PROVERBS 3:13-14, 18

Lily

A flower Jesus referred to in his teachings (Matthew 6:28-30).

You, O God, are my king from ages past, bringing salvation to the earth. You set the boundaries of the earth, and you make both summer and winter. PSALM 74:12, 17

Myrrh

A fragrant ingredient of the holy anointing oil (Exodus 30:23-33).

But thanks be to God, who made us his captives and leads us along in Christ's triumphal procession. Now wherever we go he uses us to tell others about the Lord and to spread the Good News like a sweet perfume. 2 CORINTHIANS 2:14

Myrtle

A shrub with fragrant, evergreen leaves (Isaiah 41:19).

Wisdom is a tree of life to those who embrace her; happy are those who hold her tightly. PROVERBS 3:18

Olive

One of the most valuable trees of the ancient Hebrews (Genesis 8:11).

Oh, the joys of those who do not follow the advice of the wicked, or stand around with sinners, or join in with scoffers. They are like trees planted along the riverbank, bearing fruit each season without fail. Their leaves never wither, and in all they do, they prosper. PSALM 1:1, 3

Rose of Sharon

A species of rockrose, whose flower resembles the brier rose (Song of Songs 2:1).

You, O God, are my king from ages past, bringing salvation to the earth. You set the boundaries of the earth, and you make both summer and winter. PSALM 74:12, 17

Why do you like your name?

I love my name—it's a Bible name, and you don't hear it all that often.
Sharon

Tamarisk TAM UH RISK

A soft-wooded tree of desert wadis, with small tassels of pink or white flowers (Genesis 21:33).

Wisdom is a tree of life to those who embrace her; happy are those who hold her tightly. PROVERBS 3:18

Willow

Commonly found beside perennial streams in the Middle East (Job 40:22; Isaiah 15:7).

Oh, the joys of those who do not follow the advice of the wicked, or stand around with sinners, or join in with scoffers. They are like trees planted along the riverbank, bearing fruit each season without fail. Their leaves never wither, and in all they do, they prosper. PSALM 1:1, 3

Other Bible Names

*A*lthough these names don't fit under any particular category, one of them may be the perfect name for your child! These distinctive names will give your child an interesting name with a biblical connection. If explained with careful thought, these names can hold as much spiritual significance as common Bible names like Mary and John.

*A*ngel / **Angel**

A messenger of God (1 Samuel 29:9; 2 Samuel 14:17, 20).

I will sing of the tender mercies of the LORD forever! Young and old will hear of your faithfulness. PSALM 89:1

*A*riel EHR IH EL

A name for the altar of burnt offering described by Ezekiel (Ezekiel 43:15-16).

"Hearth of God" (Hebrew)

O LORD, I have longed for your salvation, and your law is my delight. PSALM 119:174

*G*loria

"Glory to God" (Latin)

"Glory to God in the highest heaven, and peace on earth to all whom God favors." LUKE 2:14

*M*iracle

"An act of God"

Search for the Lord and for his strength, and keep on searching. Think of the wonderful works he has done, the miracles and judgments he handed down. PSALM 105:4-5

Selah SEE LUH
Musical or liturgical sign that appears seventy-one times in the book of Psalms.

I will sing of the tender mercies of the LORD forever! Young and old will hear of your faithfulness. PSALM 89:1

Seraphim SEHR UH FIM
Celestial beings with six wings (Isaiah 6).

I will sing of the tender mercies of the LORD forever! Young and old will hear of your faithfulness. PSALM 89:1

Star
The star of Bethlehem, which heralded the birth of Christ (Matthew 2).

The LORD is my light and my salvation—so why should I be afraid? The LORD protects me from danger—so why should I tremble? PSALM 27:1

Talitha TA LEE THUH
Talitha cumi ("Little girl, . . . arise") were the Aramaic words spoken by Jesus to the daughter of Jairus (Mark 5:41).

"So if the Son sets you free, you will indeed be free." JOHN 8:36

NAMES
WITH
CONNECTION

Names from Christian History

Names from Christian history can provide a unique spiritual heritage for your child. Names featured in this section reflect individuals whose contribution to religious/Christian history is substantial and has been remembered for centuries. In addition, names chosen in this section reflect current naming trends, such as the use of surnames as first names.

Names from Christian history give you—and someday your child—the opportunity to research the life of the person whose name you find intriguing. With each name in this section, you will find a short description of what the person was known for and the time period in which he or she lived. Behind each name and description lies the story of a person whose life was dedicated to serving God— an inspiration to all, especially their namesakes.

Ada

Ada R. Habershon (1861–1918). Author, teacher, and biblical scholar.

"Happy" (Teutonic)

But let all who take refuge in you rejoice; let them sing joyful praises forever. Protect them, so all who love your name may be filled with joy. PSALM 5:11

Agatha

Agatha (c. 225–251). Christian woman with unusual beauty who refused the governor of Sicily's seduction and was tortured as a result.

"Good" (Greek)

God is my shield, saving those whose hearts are true and right. PSALM 7:10

Alice

Alice Blanchard Merriam Coleman (1858–c. 1918). Home missionary to minorities, especially immigrants, in the United States. Alice H. Gregg (1893–1966). Missionary to China for thirty-five years.

"Truth" (Greek) or "of noble birth" (Old German)

But you desire honesty from the heart, so you can teach me to be wise in my inmost being. PSALM 51:6

Amalie

Amalie von Lasaulx (1815–1872). Missionary nurse and philanthropist in Germany.
"Industrious, hardworking" (German). Form of Amelia.

Work hard and cheerfully at whatever you do, as though you were working for the Lord rather than for people.
COLOSSIANS 3:23

Amanda

Amanda McFarland (c. 1837–c. 1898). She is believed to have been the first woman missionary to Alaska, establishing a home for girls trying to escape from white traders who had purchased them in exchange for goods the Eskimos desired. Amanda Smith (1837–1915). Internationally known evangelist born of slave parents in Maryland.
"Deserving of love" (Latin)

Dear friends, let us continue to love one another, for love comes from God. Anyone who loves is born of God and knows God.
1 JOHN 4:7

Ambrose

Bishop of Milan (c. 330–397). He was the first Roman church father to break away from legalism. He baptized Augustine, who made the grace of the gospel the theme of Western theology. Ambrose Jessup Tomlinson (1865–1943). Missionary to Appalachia, early leader of the Church of God.
"Divine, immortal one" (Greek)

God blesses the people who patiently endure testing. Afterward they will receive the crown of life that God has promised to those who love him. JAMES 1:12

Amelia

Amelia Hudson Taylor Broomhall (1835–1918). Beloved sister of J. Hudson Taylor, who, with her husband, operated the home office of the China Inland Mission. When her brother's wife died, she took his children to raise with hers. "Industrious, hardworking" (Teutonic)

The kings of the earth prepare for battle; the rulers plot together against the LORD and against his anointed one. PSALM 2:2

Amy / Aimee

Aimee Semple Kennedy McPherson (1890–1944). Missionary, author, evangelist, and founder of the International Church of the Four Square Gospel. Amy Carmichael (1867–1951). Missionary to India, founder of the Dohnavur Fellowship, a society devoted to saving neglected and ill-treated children. "Beloved one" (Latin)

Dear friends, let us continue to love one another, for love comes from God. Anyone who loves is born of God and knows God.
1 JOHN 4:7

Anastasia

There are many Anastasias in Christian history: (c. 25–c. 70) She is believed to have become a Christian after hearing one of Christ's disciples preach. She was martyred for her faith during Nero's persecution. (c. 230–c.259) Daughter of Constantius Chlorus. Her Christian influence in the home is credited as a major contribution to Constantine. (c. 553–580) A Greek woman who fled to Egypt after she was threatened with being forced into Emperor Justinian's harem and who lived for twenty-eight years in Egypt disguised as a monk.

THE BOOK OF NAMES

"One who shall rise again" (Greek)

How we thank God, who gives us victory over sin and death through Jesus Christ our Lord! 1 CORINTHIANS 15:57

Andrea

Andrea Gabrieli (c. 1520–1586). Organist, composer, and teacher of church music in Italy.

"Womanly, feminine" (Greek)

May all who are godly be happy in the LORD and praise his holy name! PSALM 97:12

Andreas

Andreas Bodenstein von Carlstadt (c. 1477–1541). German Protestant reformer.

"Manly" (Latin)

"I thank and praise you, God of my ancestors, for you have given me wisdom and strength. You have told me what we asked of you and revealed to us what the king demanded." DANIEL 2:23

Angela

Angela F. Newman (1837–c. 1905). Author, teacher, and pioneer missionary who worked to aid Mormon women wishing to escape from polygamy.

"Heavenly messenger" (Greek)

I will sing of the tender mercies of the LORD forever! Young and old will hear of your faithfulness. PSALM 89:1

Anna

Anna Dederer (1902–1976). Pioneer missionary evangelist and nurse in the Micronesian Islands. Anna S. Kugler

(1856–1930). Missionary doctor in India.
Anna Statler (1874–1933). Missionary to
India for twenty-two years who worked
among women, teaching them to read and
write.
"Full of grace" (Latin form of Hebrew Anne)

*I am determined to keep your principles, even
forever, to the very end.* PSALM 119:112

*W*hy do you like
your name?

I don't run into a lot
of people named
Anne, and I like the
way it "looks" on
paper.
Anne

Augustine

Aurelius Augustine (354–430). Theologian, author of *The
City of God,* and one of the greatest church Fathers of all time.
"Magnificent" (Latin)

*With all my heart I will praise you, O Lord my God. I will give
glory to your name forever.* PSALM 86:12

Baxter

Richard Baxter (1615–1691). English author, hymn writer,
and preacher who is known as one of the foremost spokesmen
of the Puritan party within the Church of England.
"Baker" (Old English). A trade name.

*"I thank and praise you, God of my ancestors, for you have given
me wisdom and strength. You have told me what we asked of you
and revealed to us what the king demanded."* DANIEL 2:23

Beryl

Beryl Elizabeth Busby (1903–1983). Outstanding missionary
to Indonesia and the Far East.
"Dazzling jewel" (Greek). A jewel name.

The LORD is my light and my salvation—so why should I be

afraid? The LORD protects me from danger—so why should I tremble? PSALM 27:1

Blake / *Blake*
William Blake (1757–1827). English Christian writer, engraver, artist, and poet.
"Black, dark" (Old English); also "pale, shining" (Old English)

"Arise, Jerusalem! Let your light shine for all the nations to see! For the glory of the LORD is shining upon you." ISAIAH 60:1

Bridget
Bridget of Sweden (c. 1303–1373). Established the Order of the Most Holy Savior in Sweden, living a life of piety and service.
"Strong" (Irish)

"I thank and praise you, God of my ancestors, for you have given me wisdom and strength. You have told me what we asked of you and revealed to us what the king demanded." DANIEL 2:23

Brilliana
Lady Brilliana Conway Harley (1600–c. 1644). Married to Sir Robert Harley, who headed the Tory ministry in 1710 and later was elected to Parliament. When she was threatened because of her testimony, she refused to surrender Brampton Castle, explaining that it was an honor to suffer for the cause of Christ.
"Brilliant"

The LORD is more pleased when we do what is just and right than when we give him sacrifices. PROVERBS 21:3

Candace

Candace (c. 25–c. 41). First-century queen of Ethiopia believed to have been converted through the testimony of her treasurer. Her conversion opened the way for Christianity to be preached throughout her kingdom. The conversion of her treasurer is recorded in Acts 8.

"Glittering, glowing white" (Latin)

When I learn your righteous laws, I will thank you by living as I should! PSALM 119:7

Carey / *Carey*

William Carey (1776–1834). Pioneer missionary to India, linguist, and agriculturist.

"From the fortess" (Celtic). A residence name

My salvation and my honor come from God alone. He is my refuge, a rock where no enemy can reach me. PSALM 62:7

Carie

Carie Green Lumbley (1869–1947). Pioneer missionary to Nigeria.

"Strong, womanly"

Don't be afraid, for I am with you. Do not be dismayed, for I am your God. I will strengthen you. I will help you. I will uphold you with my victorious right hand. ISAIAH 41:10

Carlyle

Thomas Carlyle (1795–1881). Literary figure in nineteenth-century England: biographer, social and philosophical essayist, historian, and critic.

Meaning unknown

Lead me in the right path, O LORD, or my enemies will conquer me. PSALM 5:8

Carolina

Carolina Maria Noel (1817–1877). Author and hymn writer, probably best known for her hymn "At the Name of Jesus." "Womanly" (Latin and Spanish form of Caroline)

For the LORD your God has arrived to live among you. He is a mighty savior. He will rejoice over you with great gladness. With his love, he will calm all your fears. He will exult over you by singing a happy song. ZEPHANIAH 3:17

Catherine

Catherine of Genoa (1447–1510). Affiliated with the Third Order of the Franciscans, working with the Ladies of Mercy in St. Lazarus Hospital in Genoa, Italy. She was canonized in 1737. Catherine Mumford Booth (1829–1890). Author, evangelist, and "mother" of the Salvation Army organization, as she was the wife of William Booth, its founder. Catherine LeSourd Marshall (1915–1983). Author of *A Man Called Peter,* the biography of her husband, who was the U.S. Senate chaplain Peter Marshall. The book was a New York Times best-seller for over fifty consecutive weeks in 1955. She is also the author of *Christy,* which has sold millions of copies. "Pure" (Greek)

When I learn your righteous laws, I will thank you by living as I should! PSALM 119:7

Cecile

Cecile Isherwood (1862–1905). British missionary and
founder of an orphanage in South Africa.
"Blind" (Latin)

*LORD, you know the hopes of the helpless. Surely you will listen to
their cries and comfort them.* PSALM 10:17

Cecilia

Cecilia (c. 141–177). A Christian martyr honored by
musicians and artists. Incomplete records refer to her as a
virgin who resisted marriage, but her parents planned to force
her to marry a Roman of high birth. Only hours before the
marriage, the groom, Valerianus, was converted to
Christianity. Both were martyred for their profession of
Christ.
"Blind" (Latin)

*LORD, you know the hopes of the helpless. Surely you will listen to
their cries and comfort them.* PSALM 10:17

Chalmers

James Chalmers (1841–1901). Scottish pioneer missionary
and explorer in the South Pacific islands. Thomas Chalmers
(1780–1847). Foremost minister and leader of the evangelical
party in the Church of Scotland during the first half of the
nineteenth century.
"Lord of the household" or "chamberlain" (Teutonic)

*For you bless the godly, O LORD, surrounding them with your
shield of love.* PSALM 5:12

THE BOOK OF NAMES

Chambers

Oswald Chambers (1874–1917). Lecturer, missionary, and preacher of the "deeper life." Most well known for his devotional *My Utmost for His Highest*.
Meaning unknown

But as for me, how good it is to be near God! I have made the Sovereign LORD my shelter, and I will tell everyone about the wonderful things you do. PSALM 73:28

Charlotte

Charlotte Emilia Rumohr Carey (1761–1821). Missionary and second wife of William Carey. Her highly intellectual and spiritual life was an encouragement to him, and the Carey children loved her as well. Charlotte de Bourbon (1546–1582). Christian princess of Orange. Her Christian testimony and faithfulness influenced many, especially royalty. Charlotte (Lottie) Moon (1840–1912). Born into an aristocratic family, Lottie became a dedicated missionary who served in China for forty years.
"Womanly" (French). Feminine form of Charles

Don't be afraid, for I am with you. Do not be dismayed, for I am your God. I will strengthen you. I will help you. I will uphold you with my victorious right hand. ISAIAH 41:10

Christina

Christina Mackintosh Coillard (1829–1891). Pioneer missionary to Africa. Christina Georgina Rosetti (1830–1894). Author and hymn writer born in London. "In the Bleak Mid-Winter" is probably her most familiar hymn.
"Christian" (Latin)

I follow close behind you; your strong right hand holds me securely. PSALM 63:8

Christine

Christine de Pisan (1394–1430). French author and moralist who used her writings to express her Christian moral convictions. Christine Margaret Garnett (1886–1972). Author and missionary for forty-six years in Cuba under the Southern Baptist Home Mission Board.
"Christian" (Latin)

I follow close behind you; your strong right hand holds me securely. PSALM 63:8

Christmas

Christmas Carol Kauffman (1901–1969). Born on Christmas Day, Christmas was a memorable author and city missionary in Hannibal, Missouri.
Holiday which celebrates when Jesus Christ was born

"For God so loved the world that he gave his only Son, so that everyone who believes in him will not perish but have eternal life." JOHN 3:16

Chundra

Chundra Lela (date unknown). Daughter of a Brahmin priest in the Himalaya Mountains. She saw some Christian literature in the home of a friend, read it, and later became a Christian. So thrilled was she with her new life in Christ that she became an evangelist.
Meaning unknown

I entrust my spirit into your hand. Rescue me, LORD, for you are a faithful God. PSALM 31:5

Clara / Clare

Clara A. Swain (1834–1910). Pioneer medical missionary to
India. Clara Davis Bridgman (1872–1956). Missionary and
pioneer worker among women in South Africa. Clara Wight
Guilding (1886–1974). A Canadian-born translator, teacher,
and missionary with the Africa Inland Mission. Clara Swain
(1834–1910). First woman missionary physician to India and
the non-Christian world. Clare of Assisi (1194–1253).
Brilliant and dedicated founder of the Franciscan Order of
Poor Clares. Born into an aristocratic family, Clare was reared
in a palace, taught at home, and knew the life of wealth. At
the age of sixteen, she heard St. Francis of Assisi and
dedicated her life to serving God. She was much influenced
by St. Francis and sought his counsel on spiritual matters.
"Bright" or "illustrious" (Latin)

*The LORD is my light and my salvation—so why should I be
afraid? The LORD protects me from danger—so why should I
tremble?* PSALM 27:1

Clarissa

Clarissa Danforth (1792–c. 1851). One of the first women in
America to speak as an evangelist and conduct revival meetings.
"Clear" (Latin)

*The LORD is my light and my salvation—so why should I be
afraid? The LORD protects me from danger—so why should I
tremble?* PSALM 27:1

Constance

Constance Evelyn Padwick (1886–1968). Missionary to the
Muslim world, interpreter of Islam to Western Christianity.

"Constancy, fidelity" (Latin)

I will sing of the tender mercies of the LORD forever! Young and old will hear of your faithfulness. PSALM 89:1

Constantine

Constantine (c. 285–337). First Christian emperor of the Roman Empire, ruled from 306 to 337.

"The constant, or firm of purpose" (Latin)

Reverence for the LORD is the foundation of true wisdom. The rewards of wisdom come to all who obey him. Praise his name forever! PSALM 111:10

Cornelia / Corrie

Cornelia (Corrie) ten Boom (1893–1983). Devout survivor of the Ravensbruck concentration camp during World War II and author of her autobiography, *The Hiding Place.* Cornelia (date unknown). A historic Roman matron of wifely virtues who, when reproached for her plain attire, exhibited her children, exclaiming, "These are my jewels!"

Feminine of Cornelius, which means "battle horn" (Latin), representing constant vigilance in battle

Even though I walk through the dark valley of death, I will not be afraid, for you are close beside me. Your rod and your staff protect and comfort me. PSALM 23:4

Dale

Robert William Dale (1829–1895). English Congregationalist minister, one of the great pulpiteers of his time.

"Dweller in the valley" (Teutonic). A residence name

Even though I walk through the dark valley of death, I will not be afraid, for you are close beside me. Your rod and your staff protect and comfort me. PSALM 23:4

Damien
Father Damien de Veuster (1840–1889). Roman Catholic priest and missionary who went to work in the sordid leper colonies on the islands of Hawaii and Molokai. Damien's work created an efficient and humane environment for those who suffer from leprosy.
"Day of the week" (Anglo-Saxon). "Constant" (Greek)
Reverence for the LORD is the foundation of true wisdom. The rewards of wisdom come to all who obey him. Praise his name forever! PSALM 111:10

Darby / Darby
John Nelson Darby (1800–1882). Distinguished leader among the Plymouth Brethren, Bible translator and commentator.
Meaning unknown
Happy are people of integrity, who follow the law of the LORD. PSALM 119:1

Dawson
Christopher Dawson (1889–1970). Gifted Roman Catholic scholar and historian who focused on the history of religion and its imprint on society and culture.
Meaning unknown
He will give you all you need from day to day if you live for him and make the Kingdom of God your primary concern.
MATTHEW 6:33

Denney

James Denney (1856–1917). Scottish biblical theologian and
New Testament scholar.
Meaning unknown

*I follow close behind you; your strong right hand holds me
securely.* PSALM 63:8

Dietrich

Dietrich Bonhoeffer (1906–1945). German theologian,
author, and modern Christian martyr.
Meaning unknown

*Commit everything you do to the LORD. Trust him, and he will
help you.* PSALM 37:5

Dixon

Amzi Clarence Dixon (1854–1925). American leader in the
cause of conservative theology, advocate for the
fundamentalist movement.
"Son of Dick" (Old English). Dick is a nickname for
Richard, which means "powerful ruler" (Teutonic).

*For God has not given us a spirit of fear and timidity, but of
power, love, and self-discipline.* 2 TIMOTHY 1:7

Eleanor

Eleanor Chestnut (1868–1905). A medical missionary to
China. Eleanor (1655–1720). Empress of Austria who
demonstrated her faith by her life and her compassion for the
less fortunate. She tried to help the poor by paying their bills
and giving them food.
"Light" (Greek)

The LORD is my light and my salvation—so why should I be afraid? The LORD protects me from danger—so why should I tremble? PSALM 27:1

Eli

Eli Smith (1801–1857). American missionary to the Middle East, Bible translator.
"The highest" (Hebrew)

"I command you—be strong and courageous! Do not be afraid or discouraged. For the LORD your God is with you wherever you go." JOSHUA 1:9

Elias

John Elias (1744–1841). Popular Welsh Calvinistic Methodist preacher.
"Jehovah is God" (Hebrew)

"Once again you will have all the food you want, and you will praise the LORD your God, who does these miracles for you. Never again will my people be disgraced like this. JOEL 2:26

Eliot / Elliot

John Eliot (1604–1690). Missionary to the Indians in seventeenth-century Massachusetts. T. S. Eliot (1888–1965). American-born British poet, critic, and dramatist whose Christian convictions were evident in his writing. Awarded the Nobel Prize for literature in 1948. Philip James (Jim) Elliot (1927–1956). Missionary to the Quechua tribe. He and four other missionaries were killed by members of the Auca tribe in Ecuador. Their deaths had many repercussions around the world, including the subsequent conversion of many Aucas.
French form of Elias, which means "Jehovah is God" (Hebrew)

"Once again you will have all the food you want, and you will praise the LORD your God, who does these miracles for you. Never again will my people be disgraced like this. JOEL 2:26

Eliza

Eliza Agnew (1807–1883). Believed to have been the first single woman missionary. She served in Ceylon forty years. Eliza Jane Gillett Bridgman (c. 1803–1871). She and her husband are believed to have established the first American mission in China. Eliza Davis George (1879–1979). Teacher, school founder, faithful servant, and outstanding missionary to Liberia.

Diminutive of Elizabeth, which means "God's oath" (Hebrew)

Give me understanding and I will obey your law; I will put it into practice with all my heart. PSALM 119:34

Emily

Angelina Emily Grimke (1805–1879). A Quaker abolitionist who worked to free families of slaves. Emily Chubbuck Judson (1817–1854). Professional writer and third wife of Adoniram Judson. Together, they ministered in Burma.

"Hardworking, ambitious" (Latin) or "artistic" (English)

Take delight in the LORD, and he will give you your heart's desires. PSALM 37:4

Emma

Emma Jane Bown (1858–1924). Faithful leader and pioneer social worker in the Salvation Army who worked in settlement houses, slum work, day nurseries, maternity homes for unwed mothers, and hospitals. Emma D. Lefebre Byers (1875–1946).

Significant pioneer educator and the first woman to graduate from Elkhart Institute, which became Goshen College in Indiana. Emma Darling Cushman (1865–1930). Unusually heroic missionary nurse largely responsible for saving many lives in Asia Minor.

"Whole, universal" (Old German)

For God so loved the world that he gave his only Son, so that everyone who believes in him will not perish but have eternal life.

JOHN 3:16

Emmy

Emmy Carlsson Evald (1857–1946). Described as the single most influential woman among Swedish Lutherans in the United States.

Possibly nickname for Emma.

For God so loved the world that he gave his only Son, so that everyone who believes in him will not perish but have eternal life.

JOHN 3:16

Eugenie

Eugénie de Guérin (1800–1848). French lady remembered as an author. Her writings were such a spiritual blessing to others that they went through many printings in French and later were translated into English.

"High born" (Greek)

I will sing to the LORD because he has been so good to me.

PSALM 13:6

Eva

Eva Perkins (1858–1942). An educator and missionary.
"Life" (Hebrew)

I long to obey your commandments! Renew my life with your goodness. PSALM 119:40

Evangeline

Evangeline Cory Booth (1865–1950). Author, hymn writer, evangelist, and first general of the International Salvation Army.
"Bearer of glad tidings" (Greek)

I will sing of the tender mercies of the LORD forever! Young and old will hear of your faithfulness. PSALM 89:1

Evelyne

Evelyne Constance Harris Brand (1880–1975). An outstanding missionary to southern India and mother of Dr. Paul Brand, known for his pioneering surgery and treatment of leprosy. Evelyn Christenson (1922–). Author of *What Happens When Women Pray* and a leader in the prayer movement.
"Pleasant and agreeable" (Celtic) or "light"

Your righteousness is like the mighty mountains, your justice like the ocean depths. You care for people and animals alike, O LORD.
PSALM 36:6

Fidelia

Fidelia Fiske (1816–1864). American author and missionary to the Nestorians of Persia.
"The faithful" (Latin)

But as for me, how good it is to be near God! I have made the Sovereign LORD my shelter, and I will tell everyone about the wonderful things you do. PSALM 73:28

Frances

Frances (Fanny) Jane Crosby (1820–1915). Composer who rose above her blindness and wrote over two thousand hymns, including "To God Be the Glory," "Sweet Hour of Prayer," and "All the Way My Savior Leads Me." Frances Xavier Cabrini (1850–1917). Established many schools, orphanges, convents, and hospitals across the United States. She was the first American citizen to be canonized by the Roman Catholic Church, which was done in 1946 by Pope Pius XII. Frances Ellen Watkins Harper (1825–1911). Born to free black parents, Frances was a teacher, poet, and pioneer social worker.
"Free" (Teutonic)

"So if the Son sets you free, you will indeed be free." JOHN 8:36

Griffith

John Griffith (1831–1912). Welshman sent to interior China by the London Missionary Society, translated the New Testament, Psalms, and Proverbs into Mandarin and Wenli.
Meaning unknown

Don't pretend that you love others. Really love them. Hate what is wrong. Stand on the side of the good. Love each other with genuine affection, and take delight in honoring each other.
ROMANS 12:9-10

Hansina

Hansina Christina Fogdal Hinz (c. 1803–1896). German Moravian missionary to Greenland.

Meaning unknown

I have told you this so that you will be filled with my joy. Yes, your joy will overflow! JOHN 15:11

Harris

James Rendel Harris (1852–1941). Bible scholar, archaelogist, and orientalist.

"Son of Harry" (Old English). Harry is a nickname for either Harold ("power") or Henry ("ruler of the house" German).

"I command you—be strong and courageous! Do not be afraid or discouraged. For the LORD your God is with you wherever you go." JOSHUA 1:9

Hazel

Hazel Williams Kilbourne (1894–1955). An exceptional teacher, evangelist, author, and missionary with the Oriental Missionary Society International.

"Commander" (Teutonic). The wand of the hazel tree was the symbol of authority with ancient shepherd chiefs.

How we thank God, who gives us victory over sin and death through Jesus Christ our Lord! 1 CORINTHIANS 15:57

Helen

Helen Barrett Montgomery (1861–1934). Author, translator, missions promoter, and first American woman to lead a major denomination.

"Light" (Greek)

Your righteousness is like the mighty mountains, your justice like the ocean depths. You care for people and animals alike, O LORD.

PSALM 36:6

Helena

Helena (c. 250–c. 330). Mother of Constantine whose Christian influence was evident in her son, the first Christian emperor of Rome. She visited the Holy Land and identified several biblical sights, including the holy sepulcher.
"Light" (Latin)

Your righteousness is like the mighty mountains, your justice like the ocean depths. You care for people and animals alike, O LORD.
PSALM 36:6

Isabella / Isabelle / Isobel

Isabella Bird Bishop (1831–1902). Established a missionary hospital in Nazareth and spoke out in Britain about the needs of missionaries. Isabella Graham (1742–1814). Organized a school and founded a relief group to aid orphaned children. Isobel Miller Kuhn (1901–1956). American author and missionary to China. Isabelle Thoburn (1840–1901). American missionary educator to India.
"Consecrated to God" (Spanish)

Give me understanding and I will obey your law; I will put it into practice with all my heart. PSALM 119:34

Jane

Jane Addams (1860–1935). Author and social worker, especially known as the founder of Hull House. Jane Laurie Borthwick (1813–1897). Translator of hymns into English, including "Be Still, My Soul." Lady Jane Grey (1537–1555). England's nine-day Christian queen who was martyred for her faith.
"God's gracious gift" (Hebrew). The feminine form of John.

But the LORD still waits for you to come to him so he can show

you his love and compassion. For the LORD is a faithful God.
Blessed are those who wait for him to help them. ISAIAH 30:18

Jeanette / Jeannette
Jeannette Ridlon Piccard (1895–1981). One of the first
women to be ordained to the priesthood in the Episcopal
church.
"God is gracious" (French)
But the LORD still waits for you to come to him so he can show
you his love and compassion. For the LORD is a faithful God.
Blessed are those who wait for him to help them. ISAIAH 30:18

Jeanne
Jeanne d'Albret (1528–1572). Christian queen of Navarre
and outspoken defender of Calvin and the Huguenots.
French form of Johanna or Joan, which mean "God's gracious
gift."
May the LORD smile on you and be gracious to you.
NUMBERS 6:25

Jenny / Jennie
Jenny Lind (1821–1887). Known as the "Swedish Night-
ingale," Jenny was a popular singer around the world.
A Christian, Jenny used her platform to give her testimony
for Christ. Jennie Evelyne Hussey (no date). Poet and hymn
writer, remembered for writing the words to "Lead Me to
Calvary."
"White wave" (Cornish form of Welsh)
God blesses those whose hearts are pure, for they will see God.
MATTHEW 5:8

Jerome

Jerome (c.345–c.419). Bible translator and biblical scholar best known for *The Vulgate*, the first Latin translation of the Bible.
"Of sacred name" (Greek)

Praise the LORD! Happy are those who fear the LORD. Yes, happy are those who delight in doing what he commands. PSALM 112:1

Jessie

Jessie Jones Penn-Lewis (1861–1927). A British writer and conference speaker born in South Wales.
"God exists" (Hebrew)

Once again you will have all the food you want, and you will praise the LORD your God, who does these miracles for you. Never again will my people be disgraced like this. JOEL 2:26

Jewel / *Jewel*

John Jewel (1522–1571). Bishop of Salisbury; defender of the Protestant Church of England. Exiled after England came under Roman Catholic rule. Promoted the education of poor, bright boys.
"A precious thing" or "gem" (Old French)

Wise speech is rarer and more valuable than gold and rubies.
PROVERBS 20:15

Joan

Joan of Arc (1412–1431). Peasant who became a national heroine and France's patron saint.
"God's gracious gift" (Hebrew)

But the LORD still waits for you to come to him so he can show

*you his love and compassion. For the LORD is a faithful God.
Blessed are those who wait for him to help them.* ISAIAH 30:18

Josephine
Josephine Elizabeth Butler (1828–1907). Author and pioneer
social worker concerned with the care and protection of
needy women.
Feminine form of Hebrew Joseph, which means "He shall
add."

*To you, O LORD, I lift up my soul. I trust in you, my God! Do
not let me be disgraced, or let my enemies rejoice in my defeat.*
PSALM 25:1-2

Judson
Adoniram Judson (1788–1850). First American missionary
to go to a foreign country, Burma.
"Son of Judd," a form of Jordan (Middle English)

*Those who lead blameless lives and do what is right, speaking
the truth from sincere hearts. Those who do not charge interest on
the money they lend, and who refuse to accept bribes to testify
against the innocent. Such people will stand firm forever.*
PSALM 15:2, 5

Juliana
Juliana Falconieri (1270–1341). Founder of the Roman
Catholic community of Mantellate Sisters in Italy, whose
primary purpose was one of prayer. Juliana of Norwich
(c. 1342–c. 1413). A nun of the Benedictine order in
Norwich, England, believed to have been the first English
woman to write a book on personal spiritual experiences.
Medieval form of Julia, which means "youthful."

O God, you have taught me from my earliest childhood, and I have constantly told others about the wonderful things you do.
PSALM 71:17

Justin

Justin Martyr (c. 100–165). Early Christian writer and martyr.
"The just" (Latin)

I believe in your commands; now teach me good judgment and knowledge. PSALM 119:66

Justina

Justina Friesen Wieve (1833–1916). Author, courageous immigrant, and wife of the first leader of the Krimmer Mennonite Brethren Church.
"The just or upright" (Latin). Feminine form of Justin.

I believe in your commands; now teach me good judgment and knowledge. PSALM 119:66

Karl

Karl Heim (1874–1959). German theologian. Karl Rahner (1904–1984). German Jesuit priest and scholar. Karl Rhenius (1790–1838). German missionary to India.
A German variation of Charles, which means "a man" (Latin)

"I command you—be strong and courageous! Do not be afraid or discouraged. For the LORD your God is with you wherever you go."
JOSHUA 1:9

Katharina

Katharina Zacharias Martens (1867–1929).
Russian immigrant to Canada who
experienced many difficult times during
World War I. She became a missionary
among women in Saskatchewan, Canada.
"Pure" (Greek)

When I learn your righteous laws, I will thank
you by living as I should! PSALM 119:7

Laura

Laura Smith Haviland (1808–1898).
Significant leader in organizing assistance for
slaves escaping from the South, teaching orphaned children,
and assisting wounded soldiers. Laura Askew Haygood
(1845–1900). Evangelist, missionary to China, teacher, and
school administrator.
"The laurel" (Latin)

The LORD is wonderfully good to those who wait for him and
seek him. LAMENTATIONS 3:25

Lelia

Lelia Naylor Morris (1862–1929). Author and hymnist.
She continued to write music after she became completely
blind. "The Everlasting Arms" and "Nearer, Still Nearer" are
two of her hymns.
From Laelius, the name of a famous ancient Latin clan.

But for those who are righteous, the path is not steep and rough.
You are a God of justice, and you smooth out the road ahead of
them. ISAIAH 26:7

---

*W*hy do you like your name?

I really like my name.
While various forms
of the name are
common, I've met
only a few people
who spell it the way I
do, so I feel somewhat
distinctive without
being really weird.
I also think it looks
attractive!
Kathryn

111

Lewis

C. S. Lewis (1898–1963). Christian writer and scholar, well-known author of *Mere Christianity, The Screwtape Letters,* and *The Chronicles of Narnia,* among others. Lewis Bayly (date unknown). Welsh bishop. Lewis Sperry Chafer (1871–1952). Founder and president of Dallas Theological Seminary. "Famous warrior" (German)

My salvation and my honor come from God alone. He is my refuge, a rock where no enemy can reach me.

PSALM 62:7

Lilian/Lillian

Lilian Hamer (1912–1959). English nurse and devoted missionary to Southeast Asia with the China Inland Mission. "A lily," which has long been regarded as a symbol of purity.

May the words of my mouth and the thoughts of my heart be pleasing to you, O LORD, my rock and my redeemer.

PSALM 19:14

Lillias

Lillias Horton Underwood (c. 1860–1927). Missionary physician in Korea who became the personal physician of the Korean queen and was able to witness to her.
Form of Lillian, which means "a lily"

May the words of my mouth and the thoughts of my heart be pleasing to you, O LORD, my rock and my redeemer.

PSALM 19:14

Lindsey

Lady Ann Lindsey (c. 1645–c. 1730). Countess of Rothes and faithful Christian of nobility who aided Presbyterians by allowing her palace to be a place of refuge where believers could find food and help.

"Lincoln's Island" (Old English). A place-name

For this, O LORD, I will praise you among the nations; I will sing joyfully to your name. PSALM 18:49

Louisa / Louise

Louisa Stead (c. 1850–1917). A hymnwriter and dedicated missionary to South Africa. "Tis So Sweet to Trust in Jesus" was written by Louisa. Louise Campbell (1883–1968). Missionary who founded the Kwong Yet Girls School in Meihsein, South China.

Feminine of Louis, which means "famous in battle" (Teutonic)

How we thank God, who gives us victory over sin and death through Jesus Christ our Lord! 1 CORINTHIANS 15:57

Lucy

Lucy Apsley Hutchinson (c. 1620). A British author and devout Christian of nobility. Lucy Craft Laney (1855–1933). A native of Georgia and an extraordinary leader who rose from slavery to become an influential teacher.

"Bringer of light" (Latin)

The LORD is my light and my salvation—so why should I be afraid? The LORD protects me from danger—so why should I tremble? PSALM 27:1

Mack

Alexander Mack (1679–1735). Leader of the German
Church of the Brethren.
Nickname of Mackenzie, which means "son of the wise ruler"
(Gaelic)

*Give us gladness in proportion to our former misery! Replace the
evil years with good.* PSALM 90:15

Mae/May

Mae Elizabeth Hertzler Hershey (1877–1974). Pioneer of
Christian education and a missionary to Argentina.
"Flower" or the calendar month, or short form of Mary.

*You, O God, are my king from ages past, bringing salvation to
the earth. You set the boundaries of the earth, and you make both
summer and winter.* PSALM 74:12, 17

Magdalena

Magdalena Herbert (1878–1938). Pioneer missionary to the
Comanche tribe of Oklahoma.
From the biblical town of Magdala, which means "a tower"
(Hebrew)

*What are mortals that you should think of us, mere humans that
you should care for us? You put us in charge of everything you
made, giving us authority over all things.* PSALM 8:4, 6

Marcella

Marcella (325–410). A Christian widow of a Roman family
of nobility. She turned her palace into a place of retreat for
Bible study, teaching, and Christian activities.

Feminine form of Marcus or Mark, which mean "warlike one" (Latin)

Give honor to the LORD, you angels; give honor to the LORD for his glory and strength. PSALM 29:1

Margaret

Margaret of Navarre (1492–1549). Champion of the reformed movement in France and sister of King Francis I. Margaret of Scotland (c. 1045–1093). Wife of Scottish King Malcolm Canmore. Margaret not only championed the cause of orphans, lepers, and prisoners but thought nothing of stopping to wash the feet of beggars. She was canonized in 1250.
"A pearl" (Greek)

God blesses those whose hearts are pure, for they will see God.
MATTHEW 5:8

Marguerite

Marguerite Bourgeoys (1620–1700). Founder of the first uncloistered Roman Catholic missionary group for women in the New World.
Latin form of Mary, which means "sorrow" or "bitterness" (Hebrew)

O LORD, I have longed for your salvation, and your law is my delight. PSALM 119:174

Maria

Maria Gaetana Agnesi (1718–1799). Christian intellectual of noble parents who used her wealth and knowledge to help others.
"A pearl" or "flower" (French)

*You, O God, are my king from ages past, bringing salvation to
the earth. You set the boundaries of the earth, and you make both
summer and winter.* PSALM 74:12, 17

Marie

Marie of France (c. 1140–1220). French poet whose
Christianity is revealed in her works.
French form of Mary, which means "sorrow" or "bitterness"
(Hebrew)

*O LORD, I have longed for your salvation, and your law is my
delight.* PSALM 119:174

Marilla

Marilla Baker Ingalls (1830–1895). Missionary to Burma
who had an effective ministry with Buddhist priests and
railway employees.
An elaborated form of Mary, which means "sorrow" or
"bitterness."

*O LORD, I have longed for your salvation, and your law is my
delight.* PSALM 119:174

Marshall

Peter Marshall (1902–1949). Scottish man who became chaplain of the U.S. Senate, married to Catherine LeSourd Marshall, a
well-known author of his biography, *A Man Called Peter,* which
was on the New York Times best-seller list for over fifty weeks
in 1955.
"A ruler of men" or "horse groomer" (Old French)

*My salvation and my honor come from God alone. He is my
refuge, a rock where no enemy can reach me.* PSALM 62:7

Melinda

Melinda Ebersole (1860–1933). First full-time worker for a
city mission of the Mennonite church in Chicago.
"Beautiful, pretty"

*Since we are receiving a kingdom that cannot be destroyed, let us
be thankful and please God by worshiping him with holy fear
and awe.* HEBREWS 12:28

Michi

Michi Kawai (date unknown). A Christian educator, author,
and missionary among her own people of Japan.
Meaning unknown

*He will shield you with his wings. He will shelter you with his
feathers. His faithful promises are your armor and protection.*
PSALM 91:4

Miles

Miles Coverdale (1488–1569). English Bible translator who
published a paraphrase of the Psalms in 1534 and the first
complete English Bible in 1535. (William Tyndale had
published the first English translation in 1525.)
"Merciful" (Slavic) or "soldier" (Latin)

*I follow close behind you; your strong right hand holds me
securely.* PSALM 63:8

Minnie

Minnie Susan Anderson (1892–1967). Author, teacher,
pioneer missionary to Nigeria.
"Remembrance" or "loving memory" (Teutonic)

I will sing to the LORD because he has been so good to me.
PSALM 13:6

Monica
Monica (c. 331–387). Mother of Augustine of Hippo, who wrote *Confessions*. Monica Farrell (1898–1982). An outstanding Bible teacher, evangelist, author, and missionary in Ireland and Australia.
"Counselor" (Latin)

For the LORD grants wisdom! From his mouth come knowledge and understanding. PROVERBS 2:6

Morgan / Morgan
George Campbell Morgan (1863–1945). British teacher, prolific writer, Bible teacher.
"Born by the sea" (Celtic)

Your righteousness is like the mighty mountains, your justice like the ocean depths. You care for people and animals alike, O LORD.
PSALM 36:6

Morrow
Morrow Coffey Graham (1892–1981). Influential Christian and mother of evangelist Billy Graham. Bible study and prayer were vital in the life of this great mother.
Meaning unknown

He will shield you with his wings. He will shelter you with his feathers. His faithful promises are your armor and protection.
PSALM 91:4

Nancy

Nancy Hanks Lincoln (c. 1787–1818). Christian mother of
Abraham Lincoln.

"Grace" (Hebrew)

*Since we are receiving a kingdom that cannot be destroyed, let us
be thankful and please God by worshiping him with holy fear
and awe.* HEBREWS 12:28

Nellie

Nellie Okken (1915–1983). A pioneer missionary nurse who
had a medical ministry in addition to evangelistic efforts in
Zaire and Rwanda.

"Light" (Greek)

*Your righteousness is like the mighty mountains, your justice like
the ocean depths. You care for people and animals alike, O LORD.*
PSALM 36:6

Nettie

Nettie Fowler McCormick (1835–1923). Dedicated
Christian philanthropist who made it possible for many to
study for the ministry and prepare for missionary work.

"Neat, well-shaped, tidy" (Teutonic)

*Work hard and cheerfully at whatever you do, as though you
were working for the Lord rather than for people.*
COLOSSIANS 3:23

Nona / Nonna

Nonna (c. 329–374). Devout Christian teacher and mother
of Gregory of Nazianzus.

"The ninth" (Latin) A name sometimes given to a ninth child,

if a girl. In Latin mythology, Nona was that one of the three
Fates who spun the thread of life.

*The LORD is wonderfully good to those who wait for him and
seek him.* LAMENTATIONS 3:25

Odilia

Odilia (c. 690–720). An abbess of Alsace believed to have
been blind and later healed.

"Wealthy or prosperous"

*Such people will not be overcome by evil circumstances. Those
who are righteous will be long remembered.* PSALM 112:6

Olga

Olga (c. 902–969). A Russian queen who promoted
Christianity.

"Holy" (Teutonic)

*The LORD lives! Blessed be my rock! May the God of my salvation
be exalted!* PSALM 18:46

Olive

Olive Greene (1883–1961). Author and missionary educator
to Turkey and Greece. Olive Gruen (1883–1963). Missionary
and teacher in China.

"The olive tree"

*Kind words are like honey—sweet to the soul and healthy for the
body.* PROVERBS 16:24

Olympia

Olympia Morata (1526–1555). Poet and Italian Christian of
influence.

"Heavenly" (Greek)

Who may climb the mountain of the LORD? Who may stand in his holy place? Only those whose hands and hearts are pure, who do not worship idols and never tell lies. PSALM 24:3, 4

Owen

James Owen (1645–1706). Influential Nonconformist minister. John Owen (1616–1683). Leading theologian of the Congregational churches.

"The fortunate one" or "well-born" (Welsh)

Such people will not be overcome by evil circumstances. Those who are righteous will be long remembered. They do not fear bad news; they confidently trust the LORD to care for them.

PSALM 112:6-7

Parker

Joseph Parker (1830–1902). English Congregational preacher, writer. Matthew Parker (1504–1575). Archbishop of Canterbury. Peter Parker (1804–1888). First medical missionary to China.

"Keeper of the park" (Old English). An occupation name.

Fear of the LORD teaches a person to be wise; humility precedes honor. PROVERBS 15:33

Paula

Paula (347–404). Founder of nunneries and follower of Jerome (who translated *The Vulgate*). It is said that she knew the Scripture by memory.

"Little" (Latin). Feminine form of Paul.

But as for me, how good it is to be near God! I have made the

Sovereign LORD my shelter, and I will tell everyone about the wonderful things you do. PSALM 73:28

Petra

Petra Malena Malla Moe (1863–1953). A native of Norway, Petra was strongly influenced by D. L. Moody and R. A. Torrey and became an evangelist who ministered in Africa. "Rock" (Greek)

Wait patiently for the LORD. Be brave and courageous. Yes, wait patiently for the LORD. PSALM 27:14

Ramsay

Sir William Mitchell Ramsay (1851–1939). Classical and New Testament scholar, archaelogist.
Meaning unknown

When I learn your righteous laws, I will thank you by living as I should! PSALM 119:7

Randall

Benjamin Randall (1749–1808). New England evangelist and founder of the northern branch of the Freewill Baptists. "Shield wolf" (Teutonic). The wolf was an ancient symbol of courage.

"I command you—be strong and courageous! Do not be afraid or discouraged. For the LORD your God is with you wherever you go."
JOSHUA 1:9

Renee

Renee of France (1510–1575). Distinguished Christian of noble birth who helped Protestant refugees, including John Calvin. "Born again" (French/Latin)

If you look for me in earnest, you will find me when you seek me.
JEREMIAH 29:13

Riley / *Riley*

William Bell Riley (1861–1947). Coservative Baptist minister and educator who founded three educational institutions. "Valiant" (Irish Gaelic) or "rye field" (Middle English). A place-name.

He will shield you with his wings. He will shelter you with his feathers. His faithful promises are your armor and protection.
PSALM 91:4

Rose

Rose Horton (1883–1972). Missionary known for her translation work with the Kikamba Language Committee in Africa. Rose Hawthorne Lathrop (Mother Alphonsa) (1851–1926). Wealthy daughter of Nathaniel Hawthorne, who gave up all her material possessions and devoted herself to the aid of the destitute and those suffering from cancer. Rose of Lima (1586–1617). Worked among the needy and destitute children and was canonized in 1671.
"A rose" (Latin)

But thanks be to God, who made us his captives and leads us along in Christ's triumphal procession. Now wherever we go he uses us to tell others about the Lord and to spread the Good News like a sweet perfume. 2 CORINTHIANS 2:14

Ruskin

John Ruskin (1819–1900). Christian writer, artist, and social critic in the Victorian era.
Meaning unknown

Wait patiently for the LORD. Be brave and courageous. Yes, wait patiently for the LORD. PSALM 27:14

Sambine

Sambine (c. 99–125). A notable widow in Umbria who became a Christian through the witness of her slave girl, Seraphia. Both were martyred for their faith.
Meaning unknown

Be on guard. Stand true to what you believe. Be courageous. Be strong. 1 CORINTHIANS 16:13

Scholastica

Scholastica (480–543). Twin sister of Benedict of Nursia, who founded the Benedictine order for men. Scholastica founded the Benedictine sisters, whose purpose was to educate and give medical help and charity.
Meaning unknown

Give me understanding and I will obey your law; I will put it into practice with all my heart. PSALM 119:34

Selina / Selena / Selene

Selina Hastings Huntingdon (1701–1791). A benevolent and devout Christian and originator of a Calvinistic Methodist group.
"The moon" (Greek)

Your righteousness is like the mighty mountains, your justice like the ocean depths. You care for people and animals alike, O LORD. PSALM 36:6

Selwyn / *Selwyn*

George Augustus Selwyn (1809–1878). First Anglican bishop of New Zealand.

"Palace friend" or "friend at court" (Anglo-Saxon)

Trust in the LORD with all your heart; do not depend on your own understanding. Seek his will in all you do, and he will direct your paths. PROVERBS 3:5-6

Seraphia

Seraphia (?–125). Slave girl of Antioch who witnessed to, and later converted, her mistress, Sambine, to Christianity. Both Sambine and Seraphia were martyred for their faith.

"The burning or ardent" (Hebrew)

"See, God has come to save me. I will trust in him and not be afraid. The LORD GOD is my strength and my song; he has become my salvation." ISAIAH 12:2

Sheldon

Charles Monroe Sheldon (1857–1949). American Congregational clergyman and religious publicist who wrote *In His Steps,* which has sold over six million copies.

"From the hill on the ledge" (Anglo-Saxon). A residence name.

He will give you all you need from day to day if you live for him and make the Kingdom of God your primary concern.

MATTHEW 6:33

Sidney

Mary Sidney (c. 1530–1601). A British Christian author and translator.

Derived from St. Denis, the patron saint of France.

But the LORD still waits for you to come to him so he can show you his love and compassion. For the LORD is a faithful God. Blessed are those who wait for him to help them.

ISAIAH 30:18

Sojourner

Sojourner Isabella Truth (c. 1797–1883). An outspoken preacher against slavery and for the rights of women.
"A temporary resident" (French)

How we thank God, who gives us victory over sin and death through Jesus Christ our Lord!

1 CORINTHIANS 15:57

Suora

Suora Platella Nelli (1523–1588). An Italian painter remembered especially for three of her paintings: *The Crucifixion, The Descent from the Cross,* and *Adoration of the Magi.*
Meaning unknown

For you bless the godly, O LORD, surrounding them with your shield of love. PSALM 5:12

Susanna

Susanna Ansley Wesley (1669–1742). Author, teacher, and mother of nineteen children, including John and Charles Wesley.
"A lily" (Hebrew)

For the LORD God is our light and protector. He gives us grace and glory. No good thing will the LORD withhold from those who do what is right. PSALM 84:11

Tait

Archibald Campbell Tait (1811–1882). Archbishop of Canterbury, who encouraged evangelistic efforts and began popular preaching services on Sunday nights. He also risked his own life helping others during the cholera epidemic.
"Cheerful" (Scandinavian)

With joy you will drink deeply from the fountain of salvation!

ISAIAH 12:3

Taylor / Taylor

James Hudson Taylor (1832–1905). Founder of the China Inland Mission, known for going to regions where none had ventured with the gospel, in native garb and in full dependence upon God for all his needs.
"A tailor" (Old French-Latin). An occupation name.

Don't just pretend that you love others. Really love them. Hate what is wrong. Stand on the side of the good. Love each other with genuine affection, and take delight in honoring each other.

ROMANS 12:9-10

Teresa /*Theresa*

Mother Teresa (b. 1910). Roman Catholic missionary to India, working with the "poorest of the poor." Theresa T. Buck (1912-1964). Pioneer missionary nurse who helped introduce modern nursing to African nurses.
"The harvester" (Greek)

God arms me with strength; he has made my way safe.

PSALM 18:32

Tobias

Tobias Crisp (1600–1643). Popular English preacher who emphasized that God's love was a gift, freely given and not earned.
"Goodness of the Lord" (Hebrew)

But the LORD still waits for you to come to him so he can show you his love and compassion. For the LORD is a faithful God. Blessed are those who wait for him to help them. ISAIAH 30:18

Torrence / Torrance

Thomas Forsyth Torrence (b. 1913). Scottish theologian who wrote primarily on the relationship between science and theology.
"Like a tall tower" (Irish) or "tender" (Latin)

Instead, be kind to each other, tenderhearted, forgiving one another, just as God through Christ has forgiven you.
EPHESIANS 4:32

Una

Una Roberts Lawrence (1893–1972). Author and leader of the Women's Missionary Union and Home Mission Board of the Southern Baptist Convention.
"The one" (Latin)

I know the LORD is always with me. I will not be shaken, for he is right beside me. PSALM 16:8

Vibia

Vibia Perpetua (181–203). Writer and well-educated Christian of high rank who was martyred at Carthage.
Meaning unknown

You will live in joy and peace. The mountains and hills will
burst into song, and the trees of the field will clap their hands!
ISAIAH 55:12

Victoria / Victtoria

Victtoria Colonna (1490-1549). One of the first women to
have poetry published. Her writings reflected true spiritual
insight and were inspirational to the great painter
Michelangelo.
"The victorious" (Latin)

I will sing of the tender mercies of the LORD forever! Young and
old will hear of your faithfulness. PSALM 89:1

Violet

Violet Sibusissiwe Makanya (?). Born into the Zulu tribe in
Africa, Violet became a missionary, teacher, and social worker
in South Africa.
A flower name (Old French/Latin). The violet is symbolic of
modesty from the shy habit of the woodland plant.

The Sovereign LORD, the Holy One of Israel, says, "Only in
returning to me and waiting for me will you be saved. In
quietness and confidence is your strength." ISAIAH 30:15a

Walker

Thomas Walker (1859–1912). Anglican missionary to South
India.
"He who walks in the forest" (Old English)

Happy are those who obey his decrees and search for him with all
their hearts. They do not compromise with evil, and they walk
only in his paths. PSALM 119:2-3

Wesley

John Wesley (1703–1791). English evangelist, theologian,
cofounder of Methodism. Charles Wesley (1701–1788).
Cofounder of Methodism and celebrated hymn writer,
including "A Mighty Fortress Is Our God," and "Hark! The
Herald Angels Sing."

"From the west meadow" (Old English). A residence name

*Sing about the glory of his name! Tell the world how glorious he
is.* PSALM 66:2

Zoe

Zoe (c. 255–286). Zoe's husband was a jailer in Rome and
had charge of the Christians who were facing death because
of their faith. After observing and listening to the Christians
in her husband's jail, Zoe became a Christian and immedi-
ately experienced healing from a physical disability. Her
husband witnessed the miracle and became a Christian as
well. In the end, Zoe was martyred.

"Life" (Greek). The Greek translation of the Hebrew "Eve."

*I long to obey your commandments! Renew my life with your
goodness.* PSALM 119:40

Virtue Names

*V*irtue names, while not theoretically Bible names, have a
strong history in the church. They first became fashionable
in the time of the Puritans, who wanted biblical names
which hadn't been "tainted" by the Church of Rome.
In the Puritans' search for unusual names, they unearthed
such names as Eliphalet and Bezaleel, along with the more
commonly used Aarons and Solomons. Girls especially were
often given names of Christian virtue, and stern virtues such
as Humility, Submission, and Silence were common at
that time. With the decline of Pilgrim authority, many
of the virtue names slowly passed out of use.
The list in this section reflects virtue names that are positive
and emphasize freedom rather than confinement. Having
a virtue name would, no doubt, foster that quality in
your child's life, especially when you as a
parent encourage that virtue.

Amity
"Friendly"

There are "friends" who destroy each other, but a real friend sticks closer than a brother. PROVERBS 18:24

Charity
"Benevolent, charitable, loving" (Latin)

When darkness overtakes the godly, light will come bursting in. They are generous, compassionate, and righteous.

PSALM 112:4

Chastity
"The chaste"

"I take joy in doing your will, my God, for your law is written on my heart." PSALM 40:8

Constance
"The constant, or firm of purpose" (Latin)

Without wavering, let us hold tightly to the hope we say we have, for God can be trusted to keep his promise. HEBREWS 10:23

Faith
"The believing or faithful"

I will sacrifice a voluntary offering to you; I will praise your name, O LORD, for it is good. PSALM 54:6

Grace
"The graceful" (Latin)

Now may the God of peace make you holy in every way, and may your whole spirit and soul and body be kept blameless until that day when our Lord Jesus Christ comes again.

1 THESSALONIANS 5:23

Hope
"The hopeful"

But Christ, the faithful Son, was in charge of the entire household. And we are God's household, if we keep up our courage and remain confident in our hope in Christ.

HEBREWS 3:6

Joy
"Delight" (Old French)

You will show me the way of life, granting me the joy of your presence and the pleasures of living with you forever.

PSALM 16:11

Justice / Justice
"The just"

I believe in your commands; now teach me good judgment and knowledge.

PSALM 119:66

Love
"Love"

There are three things that will endure—faith, hope, and love—and the greatest of these is love.
1 CORINTHIANS 13:13

Mercy
"The merciful or compassionate"

The LORD is merciful and gracious; he is slow to get angry and full of unfailing love.
PSALM 103:8

Merry
"Pleasant, merry"

Kind words are like honey—sweet to the soul and healthy for the body. PROVERBS 16:24

Patience
"The patient"

We also pray that you will be strengthened with his glorious power so that you will have all the patience and endurance you need. May you be filled with joy. COLOSSIANS 1:11

Peace
"The peaceful"

The LORD is my shepherd; I have everything I need. He lets me rest in green meadows; he leads me beside peaceful streams.

PSALM 23:1-2

Why do you like your name?

Growing up, my mother told me that she named me Joy because she was so happy when I was born. I didn't really see the significance of my name until I was a teenager. At that time, I was struggling with family and school issues. An older friend told me I was well-named because I was enduring tough times with grace and joy. Since then, my name has meant much more to me, and reminders from friends encourage my "Joy." I think a virtue name, if explained, can give a child a sense of heritage, belonging, and purpose.
Joy

Piety
"The pious"

*When I learn your righteous laws, I will thank
you by living as I should!* PSALM 119:7

Verity
"Truth" (Latin)

*Only those whose hands and hearts are pure, who do not worship
idols and never tell lies. They will receive the LORD's blessing and
have right standing with God their savior.* PSALM 24:4-5

Contemporary
Christian Leaders

*P*eople name their children after athletes, rock stars, and politicians—so why not look at this list of contemporaries in the Christian faith for name ideas? From musicians to evangelists to pastors, the unusual names in this list hold some interesting naming ideas.

Babbie

Babbie Mason. Christian contemporary singer.
"Foreign" (Latin)

*He will give you all you need from day to day if you live for him
and make the Kingdom of God your primary concern.*

MATTHEW 6:33

CeCe

CeCe Winans. Christian contemporary singer.
Meaning unknown

*I will sing of your love and justice. I will praise you, LORD, with
songs.* PSALM 101:1

Chapman

Gary Chapman. Christian contemporary musician and song
writer. Steven Curtis Chapman. Christian musician.
"Merchant" or "trader" (Anglo-Saxon)

*Work hard and cheerfully at whatever you do, as though you
were working for the Lord rather than for people.*

COLOSSIANS 3:23

Colson

Charles Colson. Former assistant to President Nixon, whose

dramatic conversion led to his founding of Prison Fellowship Ministries.

Possibly "Son of Cole." Cole means "coal black" (Old English).

I long to obey your commandments! Renew my life with your goodness. PSALM 119:40

Dobson

James Dobson. Author, psychologist, radio host, and founder of Focus on the Family.

From medieval given name Dobbe, a pet name for Robert, which means "shining in fame" (Old English).

The LORD is my light and my salvation—so why should I be afraid? The LORD protects me from danger—so why should I tremble? PSALM 27:1

Evans

Tony Evans. Preacher and author.

"Well-born" (Greek)

But you are not like that, for you are a chosen people. You are a kingdom of priests, God's holy nation, his very own possession. This is so you can show others the goodness of God, for he called you out of the darkness into his wonderful light. 1 PETER 2:9

Francine

Francine Rivers. Prolific fiction writer.

"Free" (Teutonic)

So Christ has really set us free. Now make sure that you stay free, and don't get tied up again in slavery to the law.
GALATIANS 5:1

Gaither

Bill and Gloria Gaither. Husband-and-wife authors and
songwriters.
Meaning unknown
*Sing about the glory of his name! Tell the world how glorious he
is.* PSALM 66:2

Graham

Billy Graham. International evangelist, writer, and religious
leader. Ruth Bell Graham. Author.
"From the gray house or home" (Old English). A residence
name.
*I will lift up a cup symbolizing his salvation; I will praise the
LORD's name for saving me.* PSALM 116:13

Hayford

Jack Hayford. Pastor and author.
Meaning unknown
*And I am sure that God, who began the good work within you,
will continue his work until it is finally finished on that day
when Christ Jesus comes back again.*
PHILIPPIANS 1:6

Janette

Janette Oke. Christian fiction author.
"God's gracious gift" (Hebrew). A form of Jane.
May the LORD smile on you and be gracious to you.
NUMBERS 6:25

Luis

Luis Palau. Evangelist and author.
Spanish form of "Louis," which means "warrior" (German).

How we thank God, who gives us victory over sin and death through Jesus Christ our Lord! 1 CORINTHIANS 15:57

MacArthur

John MacArthur. Pastor and author.
"Son of Arthur," which means "noble" (Celtic).

But you are not like that, for you are a chosen people. You are a kingdom of priests, God's holy nation, his very own possession. This is so you can show others the goodness of God, for he called you out of the darkness into his wonderful light. 1 PETER 2:9

Max

Max Lucado. Pastor and best-selling writer.
"The greatest" (Latin). From Maximilian.

Such people will not be overcome by evil circumstances. Those who are righteous will be long remembered. They do not fear bad news; they confidently trust the LORD to care for them.
PSALM 112:6-7

McDowell

Josh McDowell. Popular apologist and writer, whose book *More than a Carpenter* has sold eight million copies.

For the LORD grants wisdom! From his mouth come knowledge and understanding. PROVERBS 2:6

Meaning unknown

Stormy

Stormy Omartian. Author and fitness instructor.
"Storm"

He calmed the storm to a whisper and stilled the waves. What a blessing was that stillness as he brought them safely into harbor!

PSALM 107:29-30

Taylor / *Taylor*

Kenneth Nathaniel Taylor. Translator of *The Living Bible*, publisher, and writer.
"A tailor" (Old French-Latin). An occupation name.

Don't pretend that you love others. Really love them. Hate what is wrong. Stand on the side of the good. Love each other with genuine affection, and take delight in honoring each other.

ROMANS 12:9-10

Twila

Twila Paris. Christian contemporary singer and song writer.
"Two threads woven together" (Middle English)

All of your works will thank you, LORD, and your faithful followers will bless you. They will talk together about the glory of your kingdom; they will celebrate examples of your power.

PSALM 145:10-11

Watson

Wayne Watson. Christian musician.
"Son of Wat," Wat being a short form of Walter, which means "powerful ruler" (Old German).

"See, God has come to save me. I will trust in him and not be

143

afraid. The LORD GOD *is my strength and my song; he has become my salvation.*" ISAIAH 12:2

Wellington
Wellington Boone. Author of *Breaking Through.*
"From the prosperous estate" (Anglo-Saxon). A residence name.

True religion with contentment is great wealth. 1 TIMOTHY 6:6

Wintley / *Wintley*
Wintley Phipps. Musician and author.
Meaning unknown

And I am sure that God, who began the good work within you, will continue his work until it is finally finished on that day when Christ Jesus comes back again. PHILIPPIANS 1:6

Yancey / *Yancey*
Philip Yancey. Author of *Disappointment with God.*
Meaning unknown

Create in me a clean heart, O God. Renew a right spirit within me. PSALM 51:10

POPULAR
NAMES

The most popular names in North America today include
names from all over the world—from Ireland to Arabia.
The names selected for this section include the most
commonly used names in the 1990s.

Aaron

"Enlightened, illumined" (Hebrew)

The LORD is my light and my salvation—so why should I be afraid? The LORD protects me from danger—so why should I tremble? PSALM 27:1

Abigail / Abby

"Source of delight" (Hebrew)

Take delight in the LORD, and he will give you your heart's desires. PSALM 37:4

Adam

"Man of red earth" (Hebrew). So called because traditionally the soil from which Adam was created was red.

For we are God's masterpiece. He has created us anew in Christ Jesus, so that we can do the good things he planned for us long ago. EPHESIANS 2:10

Adrian

"Man of the seacoast" (Latin)

Your righteousness is like the mighty mountains, your justice like the ocean depths. You care for people and animals alike, O LORD. PSALM 36:6

Adriana

"Dark, rich" (Italian and Spanish)

True religion with contentment is great wealth. 1 TIMOTHY 6:6

Adrienne

"From the Adriatic." French feminine form of Latin Adrian.

He will give you all you need from day to day if you live for him and make the Kingdom of God your primary concern.
MATTHEW 6:33

Akeem

"Most wise" (Nigerian)

Fear of the LORD teaches a person to be wise; humility precedes honor. PROVERBS 15:33

Alaina / Alanna

"Rock" (Celtic)

The LORD is my rock, my fortress, and my savior; my God is my rock, in whom I find protection. He is my shield, the strength of my salvation, and my stronghold. PSALM 18:2

Alan

"Handsome, harmonious" (Celtic)

God is my shield, saving those whose hearts are true and right.
PSALM 7:10

Albert

"Of noble blood, bright" (Germanic)

But you are not like that, for you are a chosen people. You are a kingdom of priests, God's holy nation, his very own possession. This is so you can show others the goodness of God, for he called you out of the darkness into his wonderful light. 1 PETER 2:9

Alec / Alex

"Protecting men" (Greek). Short forms of Alexander.

"See, God has come to save me. I will trust in him and not be afraid. The LORD GOD is my strength and my song; he has become my salvation." ISAIAH 12:2

Alejandro

Spanish form of Alexander.

So be strong and take courage, all you who put your hope in the LORD! PSALM 31:24

Alexander

"Protecting men" (Greek)

So be strong and take courage, all you who put your hope in the LORD! PSALM 31:24

Alexandra / Alexandria

"Helper, defender" (Greek)

So be strong and take courage, all you who put your hope in the LORD! PSALM 31:24

Alexis / Alexa / Alexia

"Helper, defender" (Greek)

So be strong and take courage, all you who put your hope in the LORD! PSALM 31:24

Ali

"Of noble kind" (Old German). Short form of Alice and Allison.

The Sovereign LORD is my strength! He will make me as surefooted as a deer and bring me safely over the mountains.
HABAKKUK 3:19

Alicia

Latin form of Adelhaide, which means "of noble kind."

But you are not like that, for you are a chosen people. You are a kingdom of priests, God's holy nation, his very own possession. This is so you can show others the goodness of God, for he called you out of the darkness into his wonderful light. 1 PETER 2:9

Alisa

Russian form of Alice, which means "of noble kind."

But you are not like that, for you are a chosen people. You are a kingdom of priests, God's holy nation, his very own possession. This is so you can show others the goodness of God, for he called you out of the darkness into his wonderful light. 1 PETER 2:9

Allison / Allyson

"Of noble kind" (Old French). Diminutive forms of Alice.

But you are not like that, for you are a chosen people. You are a kingdom of priests, God's holy nation, his very own possession. This is so you can show others the goodness of God, for he called you out of the darkness into his wonderful light. 1 PETER 2:9

Alyssa / Alissa

"Of noble kind." Forms of Alice.

But you are not like that, for you are a chosen people. You are a kingdom of priests, God's holy nation, his very own possession. This is so you can show others the goodness of God, for he called you out of the darkness into his wonderful light. 1 PETER 2:9

Amanda

"Deserving of love" (Latin)

Dear friends, let us continue to love one another, for love comes from God. Anyone who loves is born of God and knows God. 1 JOHN 4:7

Amber

"Amber" (Arabic). A yellow or green fossil resin used to make jewelry.

When that day arrives, the LORD their God will rescue his people, just as a shepherd rescues his sheep. They will sparkle in his land like jewels in a crown. How wonderful and beautiful they will be! The young men and women will thrive on the abundance of grain and new wine. ZECHARIAH 9:16-17

Amelia

"Hard working" (Teutonic)

Work hard and cheerfully at whatever you do, as though you were working for the Lord rather than for people. COLOSSIANS 3:23

Amy

"Beloved" (French)

Let love be your highest goal, but also desire the special abilities the Spirit gives. 1 CORINTHIANS 14:1

Anastasia
"One who shall rise again" (Greek)

How we thank God, who gives us victory over sin and death through Jesus Christ our Lord! 1 CORINTHIANS 15:57

Andre
French form of Andrew, which means "strong, manly." (Greek)

"I thank and praise you, God of my ancestors, for you have given me wisdom and strength. You have told me what we asked of you and revealed to us what the king demanded." DANIEL 2:23

Andrea
"Womanly" (Greek). A feminine form of Andrew.

May all who are godly be happy in the LORD and praise his holy name! PSALM 97:12

Andrew
"Strong, manly" (Greek)

"I thank and praise you, God of my ancestors, for you have given me wisdom and strength. You have told me what we asked of you and revealed to us what the king demanded." DANIEL 2:23

Angel / *Angel*
"God's messenger" (Hebrew)

I will sing of the tender mercies of the LORD forever! Young and old will hear of your faithfulness. PSALM 89:1

Angela / *Angelia* / *Angelina*
"God's messenger"

I will sing of the tender mercies of the LORD forever! Young and old will hear of your faithfulness. PSALM 89:1

Angelica
"Angelic" (Latin)

I will sing of the tender mercies of the LORD forever! Young and old will hear of your faithfulness. PSALM 89:1

Anna
"Graceful one" (Hebrew)

I am determined to keep your principles, even forever, to the very end. PSALM 119:112

Anne/Annie
"Graceful one" (Hebrew)

I am determined to keep your principles, even forever, to the very end. PSALM 119:112

Anthony
"Priceless" (Latin)

God saved you by his special favor when you believed. And you can't take credit for this; it is a gift from God. EPHESIANS 2:8

Antoine
French form of Anthony, which means "priceless" (Latin).

God saved you by his special favor when you believed. And you can't take credit for this; it is a gift from God. EPHESIANS 2:8

Antonio
Spanish and Italian form of Anthony.

God saved you by his special favor when you believed. And you can't take credit for this; it is a gift from God. EPHESIANS 2:8

April
"Ready to receive the sun" (Latin)

"For God so loved the world that he gave his only Son, so that everyone who believes in him will not perish but have eternal life. JOHN 3:16

Ariana
"Very holy one" (Latin)

But you are not like that, for you are a chosen people. You are a kingdom of priests, God's holy nation, his very own possession. This is so you can show others the goodness of God, for he called you out of the darkness into his wonderful light. 1 PETER 2:9

Ariel / Arielle
"Hearth of God" (Hebrew)

O LORD, I have longed for your salvation, and your law is my delight. PSALM 119:174

Arthur
"Noble" (Celtic)

But you are not like that, for you are a chosen people. You are a kingdom of priests, God's holy nation, his very own possession. This is so you can show others the goodness of God, for he called you out of the darkness into his wonderful light. 1 PETER 2:9

Ashley
"From the ash meadow" (Old English)

I waited patiently for the LORD to help me, and he turned to me and heard my cry. He lifted me out of the pit of despair, out of the mud and the mire. He set my feet on solid ground and steadied me as I walked along. PSALM 40:1-2

Ashton / *Ashton*
"Ash tree farm" (English) A place-name.

For God is the one who gives seed to the farmer and then bread to eat. In the same way, he will give you many opportunities to do good, and he will produce a great harvest of generosity in you. 2 CORINTHIANS 9:10

Asia
Name of the continent, from a Greek word meaning "east."

Praise the LORD, I tell myself; and never forget the good things he does for me. He has removed our rebellious acts as far away from us as the east is from the west. PSALM 103:2, 12

Aubrey
"Blonde ruler" (Old French)

My salvation and my honor come from God alone. He is my refuge, a rock where no enemy can reach me. PSALM 62:7

Audrey
"Noble strength" (Old English)

But you are not like that, for you are a chosen people. You are a kingdom of priests, God's holy nation, his very own possession. This is so you can show others the goodness of God, for he called you out of the darkness into his wonderful light. 1 PETER 2:9

Austin
"One who is helpful" (Latin)

The LORD is more pleased when we do what is just and right than when we give him sacrifices. PROVERBS 21:3

Autumn
"Autumn," the season

There is a time for everything, a season for every activity under heaven. ECCLESIASTES 3:1

Bailey
"Manager, local official" or "wall of the outer court of a castle" (Old French)

Take delight in the LORD, and he will give you your heart's desires. PSALM 37:4

Barbara
"Strange, foreign" (Greek)

He will give you all you need from day to day if you live for him and make the Kingdom of God your primary concern.
MATTHEW 6:33

Barry
"Spear" (Irish)

As for God, his way is perfect. All the LORD's promises prove true. He is a shield for all who look to him for protection.
PSALM 18:30

Beau
"Handsome" (French)

*When that day arrives, the LORD their God will rescue his
people, just as a shepherd rescues his sheep. They will sparkle in
his land like jewels in a crown. How wonderful and beautiful
they will be! The young men and women will thrive on the
abundance of grain and new wine.* ZECHARIAH 9:16-17

Benjamin
"Son of my right hand" (Hebrew)

*LORD, don't hold back your tender mercies from me. My only
hope is in your unfailing love and faithfulness.* PSALM 40:11

Bethany
"Worshiper of God" or "House of poverty" (Aramaic). A
biblical place-name.

*I am praying to you because I know you will answer, O God.
Bend down and listen as I pray.* PSALM 17:6

Bianca
"White" (Italian)

*Purify me from my sins, and I will be clean; wash me, and I will
be whiter than snow.* PSALM 51:7

Bill /Billy
Forms of William

*For the LORD God is our light and protector. He gives us grace
and glory. No good thing will the LORD withhold from those who
do what is right.* PSALM 84:11

Blaine
"Yellow" (Scots Gaelic)

157

He will give you all you need from day to day if you live for him and make the Kingdom of God your primary concern.
MATTHEW 6:33

Blair / **Blair**
"Plains" (Celtic). A place-name.

The LORD is my shepherd; I have everything I need. He lets me rest in green meadows; he leads me beside peaceful streams.
PSALM 23:1-2

Blake
"Black, dark" or "pale, shining" (Old English)

"Arise, Jerusalem! Let your light shine for all the nations to see! For the glory of the LORD is shining upon you."
ISAIAH 60:1

Bobby
Form of Robert, which means "shining in fame" (Old English).

The LORD is my light and my salvation—so why should I be afraid? The LORD protects me from danger—so why should I tremble? PSALM 27:1

Braden
"Salmon" (Irish Gaelic)

"Come, be my disciples, and I will show you how to fish for people!" MARK 1:17

Bradley
"Broad meadow" (Old English)

The LORD is my shepherd; I have everything I need. He lets me rest in green meadows; he leads me beside peaceful streams.

PSALM 23:1-2

Brady
"Spirited one" (Gaelic)

With joy you will drink deeply from the fountain of salvation!

ISAIAH 12:3

Brandi
"Burnt wine" (Dutch) or feminine form of Brandon.

The Spirit and the bride say, "Come." Let each one who hears them say, "Come." Let the thirsty ones come—anyone who wants to. Let them come and drink the water of life without charge.

REVELATION 22:17

Brandon
"Quick sword" (Anglo-Saxon)

God is my shield, saving those whose hearts are true and right.

PSALM 7:10

Breanne
"Strong" and "grace." A modern form of Bree and Anna.

But as for me, how good it is to be near God! I have made the Sovereign LORD my shelter, and I will tell everyone about the wonderful things you do.

PSALM 73:28

Brenda
"Flame" (Germanic)

I will delight in your principles and not forget your word.
PSALM 119:16

Brendan
"Prince" (Old Welsh)

But you are not like that, for you are a chosen people. You are a kingdom of priests, God's holy nation, his very own possession. This is so you can show others the goodness of God, for he called you out of the darkness into his wonderful light. 1 PETER 2:9

Brennan
"Drop of water, tear" (Irish Gaelic)

I waited patiently for the LORD to help me, and he turned to me and heard my cry. PSALM 40:1

Brent
"Burnt" (Old English)

O LORD, I have longed for your salvation, and your law is my delight. PSALM 119:174

Brett
"A native of Brittany" (French)

He will give you all you need from day to day if you live for him and make the Kingdom of God your primary concern.
MATTHEW 6:33

Brian / Bryan
"High, noble" (Celtic)

But you are not like that, for you are a chosen people. You are a kingdom of priests, God's holy nation, his very own possession.

This is so you can show others the goodness of God, for he called you out of the darkness into his wonderful light. 1 PETER 2:9

Brianna/Breanna

"Strong" and "grace." A modern form of Bree and Anna.

But as for me, how good it is to be near God! I have made the Sovereign LORD my shelter, and I will tell everyone about the wonderful things you do. PSALM 73:28

Brianne

"High, noble" (Celtic). Feminine form of Brian.

So be strong and take courage, all you who put your hope in the LORD! PSALM 31:24

Bridget

"Strong" (Irish)

"I thank and praise you, God of my ancestors, for you have given me wisdom and strength. You have told me what we asked of you and revealed to us what the king demanded."

DANIEL 2:23

Brittany

"One from Britain" (Latin)

"I thank and praise you, God of my ancestors, for you have given me wisdom and strength. You have told me what we asked of you and revealed to us what the king demanded."

DANIEL 2:23

Why do you like your name?

I like my name because it's a good name. I'm glad I don't have a goofy name.
Brandon

161

Brock

"Badger" (Gaelic)

For we are God's masterpiece. He has created us anew in Christ Jesus, so that we can do the good things he planned for us long ago. EPHESIANS 2:10

Brooke

"Brook, stream" (Old English)

"If you believe in me, come and drink! For the Scriptures declare that rivers of living water will flow out from within." JOHN 7:38

Bruce

"Brushwood thicket" (Scottish)

Sing to the LORD, all you godly ones! Praise his holy name. Your favor, O LORD, made me as secure as a mountain.

PSALM 30:4, 7

Bryant

Form of Brian, which means "high, noble" (Celtic).

But you are not like that, for you are a chosen people. You are a kingdom of priests, God's holy nation, his very own possession. This is so you can show others the goodness of God, for he called you out of the darkness into his wonderful light. 1 PETER 2:9

Bryce/Brice

Meaning unknown. Celtic name of fifth-century saint.

He will give you all you need from day to day if you live for him and make the Kingdom of God your primary concern.

MATTHEW 6:33

Byron
"Cowshed" (Old English)

Sing to the LORD, all you godly ones! Praise his holy name. Your favor, O LORD, made me as secure as a mountain.

PSALM 30:4, 7

Caitlin/Kaitlyn
"Pure" (Irish Gaelic). Forms of Katherine.

When I learn your righteous laws, I will thank you by living as I should! PSALM 119:7

Caleb
"Bold, impetuous" or "dog" (Hebrew), signifying faithful affection.

The steps of the godly are directed by the LORD. He delights in every detail of their lives.

PSALM 37:23

Callie
"Beautiful voice" (Greek)

May the words of my mouth and the thoughts of my heart be pleasing to you, O LORD, my rock and my redeemer.

PSALM 19:14

Calvin
"Bald" (Latin)

I long to obey your commandments! Renew my life with your goodness. PSALM 119:40

Cameron

"Crooked hill" (Scottish) or "a field" (French)

He will give you all you need from day to day if you live for him and make the Kingdom of God your primary concern.

MATTHEW 6:33

Camille

"Virginlike" or "innocent" (Latin)

God blesses those whose hearts are pure, for they will see God.

MATTHEW 5:8

Candace

"Incandescent, full of light, glowing" (Greek)

The LORD is my light and my salvation—so why should I be afraid? The LORD protects me from danger—so why should I tremble? PSALM 27:1

Carissa

"Grace" (Greek) or "little dear one" (Italian)

Now may the God of peace make you holy in every way, and may your whole spirit and soul and body be kept blameless until that day when our Lord Jesus Christ comes again.

1 THESSALONIANS 5:23

Carl

"Farmer" (Teutonic) or "high, noble" (Celtic)

For God is the one who gives seed to the farmer and then bread

to eat. In the same way, he will give you many opportunities to do good, and he will produce a great harvest of generosity in you.
2 CORINTHIANS 9:10

Carlos
Spanish form of Charles, which means "a man" (Anglo-Saxon).

For we are God's masterpiece. He has created us anew in Christ Jesus, so that we can do the good things he planned for us long ago. EPHESIANS 2:10

Carly
"Womanly" (Old German). Feminine form of Carl.

Charm is deceptive, and beauty does not last; but a woman who fears the LORD will be greatly praised.
PROVERBS 31:31

Carmen
"The garden" (Hebrew)

My job was to plant the seed in your hearts, and Apollos watered it, but it was God, not we, who made it grow. The ones who do the planting or watering aren't important, but God is important because he is the one who makes the seed grow.
1 CORINTHIANS 3:6-7

Carolina / Caroline / Carolyn
"Womanly"

Charm is deceptive, and beauty does not last; but a woman who fears the LORD will be greatly praised. PROVERBS 31:30

Carrie
"Womanly." A form of Caroline.

Charm is deceptive, and beauty does not last; but a woman who fears the LORD will be greatly praised. PROVERBS 31:30

Casey / Casey
"Brave" (Celtic)

Wait patiently for the LORD. Be brave and courageous. Yes, wait patiently for the LORD. PSALM 27:14

Cassandra
Prophetess in ancient Troy (Greek)

Trust in the LORD with all your heart; do not depend on your own understanding. Seek his will in all you do, and he will direct your paths. PROVERBS 3:5-6

Cassidy
Surname of unknown meaning (Irish Gaelic)

"I thank and praise you, God of my ancestors, for you have given me wisdom and strength. You have told me what we asked of you and revealed to us what the king demanded." DANIEL 2:23

Cassie
Form of Cassandra

Trust in the LORD with all your heart; do not depend on your own understanding. Seek his will in all you do, and he will direct your paths. PROVERBS 3:5-6

Catherine (see Katherine)

Cedric
"Chief" (Old English)

The LORD is my shepherd; I have everything I need. He lets me rest in green meadows; he leads me beside peaceful streams.

PSALM 23:1-2

Chad
"Warrior" (Celtic)

"I command you—be strong and courageous! Do not be afraid or discouraged. For the LORD your God is with you wherever you go." JOSHUA 1:9

Chance
Short form of Chauncey, which means "chancellor" (Latin).

He will give you all you need from day to day if you live for him and make the Kingdom of God your primary concern.

MATTHEW 6:33

Chanel
Surname (French)

"I thank and praise you, God of my ancestors, for you have given me wisdom and strength. You have told me what we asked of you and revealed to us what the king demanded." DANIEL 2:23

Chantel
American version of the French Chantal, which means "stone, stony place."

My salvation and my honor come from God alone. He is my refuge, a rock where no enemy can reach me. PSALM 62:7

Charlene

"Womanly." A feminine form of Charles.

Charm is deceptive, and beauty does not last; but a woman who fears the LORD will be greatly praised. PROVERBS 31:30

Charles / Charlie

"A man" (Anglo-Saxon)

For we are God's masterpiece. He has created us anew in Christ Jesus, so that we can do the good things he planned for us long ago. EPHESIANS 2:10

Charlotte

"Womanly." A French feminine form of Charles.

Charm is deceptive, and beauty does not last; but a woman who fears the LORD will be greatly praised. PROVERBS 31:30

Chase

"Hunter" (Old French)

To you, O LORD, I lift up my soul. I trust in you, my God! Do not let me be disgraced, or let my enemies rejoice in my defeat. PSALM 25:1-2

Chasity / Chastity

"Sexual purity" (Latin)

Only those whose hands and hearts are pure, who do not worship idols and never tell lies. They will receive the LORD's blessing and have right standing with God their savior. PSALM 24:4-5

Chelsea

"Harbor" (Old English)

Your righteousness is like the mighty mountains, your justice like the ocean depths. You care for people and animals alike, O LORD.
PSALM 36:6

Cheyenne
Native American nation

He will give you all you need from day to day if you live for him and make the Kingdom of God your primary concern.
MATTHEW 6:33

Chloe
"Green, young plant" (Greek)

O God, you have taught me from my earliest childhood, and I have constantly told others about the wonderful things you do.
PSALM 71:17

Christian / Christian
"Follower of Christ" (Latin)

Live in such a way that God's love can bless you as you wait for the eternal life that our Lord Jesus Christ in his mercy is going to give you. JUDE 1:21

Christina / Christine
"Christ-bearer" (Latin). French feminine form of Christian.

Live in such a way that God's love can bless you as you wait for the eternal life that our Lord Jesus Christ in his mercy is going to give you. JUDE 1:21

Christopher
"Christ-bearer" (Greek)

I follow close behind you; your strong right hand holds me securely. PSALM 63:8

Ciara
Possibly "Dark" (Irish)

Trust in the LORD with all your heart; do not depend on your own understanding. Seek his will in all you do, and he will direct your paths. PROVERBS 3:5-6

Claire
"Bright or illustrious" (French)

The LORD is my light and my salvation—so why should I be afraid? The LORD protects me from danger—so why should I tremble? PSALM 27:1

Clayton
"Of the earth" (Old English)

"O Israel, can I not do to you as this potter has done to his clay? As the clay is in the potter's hand, so are you in my hand." JEREMIAH 18:6

Clifford
"Ford at the cliff" (Old English)

"If you believe in me, come and drink! For the Scriptures declare that rivers of living water will flow out from within." JOHN 7:38

Clinton
"Hill town" (English). A place-name.

He will give you all you need from day to day if you live for him
and make the Kingdom of God your primary concern.
MATTHEW 6:33

Cody
From Irish Gaelic *Mac Oda;* "riches" (Old German)
True religion with contentment is great wealth. 1 TIMOTHY 6:6

Cole
"Coal black" (Old English)
I long to obey your commandments! Renew my life with your
goodness. PSALM 119:40

Colin
"Youth" (Scots Gaelic)
O God, you have taught me from my earliest childhood, and I
have constantly told others about the wonderful things you do.
PSALM 71:17

Colleen
"Girl" (Irish Gaelic)
O God, you have taught me from my earliest childhood, and I
have constantly told others about the wonderful things you do.
PSALM 71:17

Colton
"Coal town" (Old English)
I long to obey your commandments! Renew my life with your
goodness. PSALM 119:40

Connor
"Wolf lover" (Irish Gaelic)

He will shield you with his wings. He will shelter you with his feathers. His faithful promises are your armor and protection.

PSALM 91:4

Corey
"Mountain glen" or "ravine" (Scottish)

Sing to the LORD, all you godly ones! Praise his holy name. Your favor, O LORD, made me as secure as a mountain.

PSALM 30:4, 7

Cori
"Girl" (Greek)

O God, you have taught me from my earliest childhood, and I have constantly told others about the wonderful things you do.

PSALM 71:17

Corinne
"Girl" (Greek)

O God, you have taught me from my earliest childhood, and I have constantly told others about the wonderful things you do.

PSALM 71:17

Coty / Coty
"Old house" (French surname)

"I will show you what it's like when someone comes to me, listens to my teaching, and then obeys me. It is like a person who builds a house on a strong foundation laid upon the underlying rock.

When the floodwaters rise and break against the house, it stands firm because it is well built." LUKE 6:47-48

Courtney / Courtney

"Of the court" (French)

"I thank and praise you, God of my ancestors, for you have given me wisdom and strength. You have told me what we asked of you and revealed to us what the king demanded." DANIEL 2:23

Craig

"Crag" (Celtic)

He makes me as surefooted as a deer, leading me safely along the mountain heights. PSALM 18:33

Crystal

"Ice or translucent glass, clear" (Greek)

Now we see things imperfectly as in a poor mirror, but then we will see everything with perfect clarity. All that I know now is partial and incomplete, but then I will know everything completely, just as God knows me now. 1 CORINTHIANS 13:12

Curtis

"Courteous" (Old French)

Do for others as you would like them to do for you. LUKE 6:31

Cynthia

Title of the Greek moon goddess

His dynasty will go on forever; his throne is as secure as the sun, as eternal as the moon, my faithful witness in the sky!

PSALM 89:36-37

Dakota / *Dakota*

Name of a Native American nation

He will give you all you need from day to day if you live for him and make the Kingdom of God your primary concern.

MATTHEW 6:33

Dale

"Valley" (Old English)

Even when I walk through the dark valley of death, I will not be afraid, for you are close beside me. Your rod and your staff protect and comfort me. PSALM 23:4

Dallas

"Wise" (Gaelic)

Fear of the LORD teaches a person to be wise; humility precedes honor. PROVERBS 15:33

Dalton

"Valley farm" (Old English)

But as for me, how good it is to be near God! I have made the Sovereign LORD my shelter, and I will tell everyone about the wonderful things you do. PSALM 73:28

Damian / Damien

"To tame" (Greek)

"Take my yoke upon you. Let me teach you, because I am humble and gentle, and you will find rest for your souls."

MATTHEW 11:29

Damon

Greek form of Damian.

"Take my yoke upon you. Let me teach you, because I am humble and gentle, and you will find rest for your souls."
MATTHEW 11:29

Dana / *Dana*

"From Denmark" (Old English)

Trust in the LORD with all your heart; do not depend on your own understanding. Seek his will in all you do, and he will direct your paths. PROVERBS 3:5-6

Dane

"A Dane" (Middle English)

For you bless the godly, O LORD, surrounding them with your shield of love. PSALM 5:12

Daniel

"God is my judge" (Hebrew)

God is my shield, saving those whose hearts are true and right.
PSALM 7:10

Danielle

"God is my judge" (Hebrew). Feminine form of Daniel.

God is my shield, saving those whose hearts are true and right.
PSALM 7:10

Danny

Form of Daniel, which means "God is my judge" (Hebrew).

God is my shield, saving those whose hearts are true and right.
PSALM 7:10

Darius
"He who upholds the good" (Persian)

*For God is the one who gives seed to the farmer and then bread
to eat. In the same way, he will give you many opportunities to
do good, and he will produce a great harvest of generosity in you.*
2 CORINTHIANS 9:10

Darren
"Black oak" (Irish Gaelic)

*Darkness as black as night will cover all the nations of the earth,
but the glory of the LORD will shine over you.* ISAIAH 60:2

Darrion / Darian
"Wealthy" (Persian)

True religion with contentment is great wealth. 1 TIMOTHY 6:6

Darryl
"Beloved" (French)

*Dear friends, let us continue to love one another, for love comes
from God. Anyone who loves is born of God and knows God.*
1 JOHN 4:7

David
"Beloved" (Hebrew)

*Dear friends, let us continue to love one another, for love comes
from God. Anyone who loves is born of God and knows God.*
1 JOHN 4:7

Dawn
"Daybreak" (Old English)

Let me hear of your unfailing love to me in the morning, for I am trusting you. Show me where to walk, for I have come to you in prayer. PSALM 143:8

Dean
"Chief of ten" (Middle English)

God is my shield, saving those whose hearts are true and right. PSALM 7:10

DeAndre
Meaning unknown (African American)

He will give you all you need from day to day if you live for him and make the Kingdom of God your primary concern. MATTHEW 6:33

Deanna
A variation of Dianna, which means "the archer, divine, or divine goddess of the hunt" (Latin).

Darkness as black as night will cover all the nations of the earth, but the glory of the LORD will shine over you. ISAIAH 60:2

Deborah
"Bee, wasp" (Hebrew). In ancient Egypt, the bee was a symbol of regal power.

Instead, I want to see a mighty flood of justice, a river of righteous living that will never run dry. AMOS 5:24

Demetrius

From the goddess of fertility, Demeter (Greek).

I am determined to keep your principles, even forever, to the very end. PSALM 119:112

Denise

French feminine form of Dennis, which means "the god of wine."

The Spirit and the bride say, "Come." Let each one who hears them say, "Come." Let the thirsty ones come—anyone who wants to. Let them come and drink the water of life without charge.
REVELATION 22:17

Dennis

From Dionysus, the god of food and wine (Greek).

The Spirit and the bride say, "Come." Let each one who hears them say, "Come." Let the thirsty ones come—anyone who wants to. Let them come and drink the water of life without charge.
REVELATION 22:17

Deontae

Meaning unknown (African American)

I will lift up a cup symbolizing his salvation; I will praise the LORD's name for saving me. PSALM 116:13

Derek

"A great ruler" (Teutonic)

God is my shield, saving those whose hearts are true and right.
PSALM 7:10

Desiree
"Desired one" (French)

Dear friends, let us continue to love one another, for love comes from God. Anyone who loves is born of God and knows God.
1 JOHN 5:7

Desmond
"Man from South Munster" (Irish Gaelic)

For we are God's masterpiece. He has created us anew in Christ Jesus, so that we can do the good things he planned for us long ago. EPHESIANS 2:10

Destiny
"Fortune, fate" (Latin)

"For I know the plans I have for you," says the LORD. "They are plans for good and not for disaster, to give you a future and a hope." JEREMIAH 29:11

Devin
"Fawn" (Irish Gaelic)

As the deer pants for streams of water, so I long for you, O God.
PSALM 42:1

Devon
English county name

He will give you all you need from day to day if you live for him and make the Kingdom of God your primary concern.
MATTHEW 6:33

Diana / Diane
Roman goddess of the moon

His dynasty will go on forever; his throne is as secure as the sun, as eternal as the moon, my faithful witness in the sky!
PSALM 89:36-37

Dominic / Dominque
"Of the Lord" (Latin)

Those who lead blameless lives and do what is right, speaking the truth from sincere hearts. Those who do not charge interest on the money they lend, and who refuse to accept bribes to testify against the innocent. Such people will stand firm forever. PSALM 15:2, 5

Dominique
French feminine form of Dominic, which means "belonging to the Lord" (Latin).

The LORD is wonderfully good to those who wait for him and seek him. LAMENTATIONS 3:25

Donald
"World mighty" (Scots Gaelic)

He will give you all you need from day to day if you live for him and make the Kingdom of God your primary concern.
MATTHEW 6:33

Donovan
"Dark warrior" (Gaelic)

Darkness as black as night will cover all the nations of the earth, but the glory of the LORD will shine over you. ISAIAH 60:2

Donte / Dante
"Lasting" (Italian)

His anger lasts for a moment, but his favor lasts a lifetime! Weeping may go on all night, but joy comes with the morning. PSALM 30:5

Douglas
"The dark sea" (Scottish)

Darkness as black as night will cover all the nations of the earth, but the glory of the LORD will shine over you. ISAIAH 60:2

Drew
"To carry" (Old German)

"Take my yoke upon you. Let me teach you, because I am humble and gentle, and you will find rest for your souls."
MATTHEW 11:29

Dustin
"Dusty place" (English). A place-name.

Fear of the LORD teaches a person to be wise; humility precedes honor. PROVERBS 15:33

Dwayne / Duane
"Black" (Irish Gaelic)

Darkness as black as night will cover all the nations of the earth, but the glory of the LORD will shine over you. ISAIAH 60:2

Dylan
"Of the sea" (Welsh)

*W*hy do you like your name?

It fits me! It's different, and there are usually not too many Duanes in a room.
Duane

Your righteousness is like the mighty mountains, your justice like the ocean depths. You care for people and animals alike, O LORD.
PSALM 36:6

Ebony
"Black" (Middle English)

Darkness as black as night will cover all the nations of the earth, but the glory of the LORD will shine over you. ISAIAH 60:2

Edward / Eddie
"Happy protector" (Old English)

Take my yoke upon you. Let me teach you, because I am humble and gentle, and you will find rest for your souls.
MATTHEW 11:29

Edwin
"Wealthy friend" (Old English)

True religion with contentment is great wealth. 1 TIMOTHY 6:6

Elijah
"Jehovah is God" (Hebrew)

Once again you will have all the food you want, and you will praise the LORD your God, who does these miracles for you. Never again will my people be disgraced like this. JOEL 2:26

Elisa / Elise
French form of Elizabeth, which means "God's oath."

Give me understanding and I will obey your law; I will put it into practice with all my heart. PSALM 119:34

Elizabeth
"God's oath" (Hebrew)

Give me understanding and I will obey your law; I will put it into practice with all my heart. PSALM 119:34

Ellen
"Mercy or merciful" (French)

So let us come boldly to the throne of our gracious God. There we will receive his mercy, and we will find grace to help us when we need it. HEBREWS 4:16

Elliott
French form of Elias, which means "Jehovah is God" (Hebrew).

Once again you will have all the food you want, and you will praise the LORD your God, who does these miracles for you. Never again will my people be disgraced like this. JOEL 2:26

Emily
"Hardworking, ambitious" (Latin) or "artistic" (English)

Take delight in the LORD, and he will give you your heart's desires. PSALM 37:4

Emma
"Whole, universal" (Old German)

For God so loved the world that he gave his only Son, so that everyone who believes in him will not perish but have eternal life. JOHN 3:16

Emmanuel / *Emmanuelle*

"God is with us" (Hebrew)

For I can do everything with the help of Christ who gives me the strength I need. PHILIPPIANS 4:13

Eric

"Ever powerful" (Scandinavian)

But as for me, how good it is to be near God! I have made the Sovereign LORD my shelter, and I will tell everyone about the wonderful things you do. PSALM 73:28

Erica

Feminine form of Eric, which means "ever powerful" (Scandinavian).

But as for me, how good it is to be near God! I have made the Sovereign LORD my shelter, and I will tell everyone about the wonderful things you do. PSALM 73:28

Erin

Poetic name for Ireland

The LORD is my shepherd; I have everything I need. He lets me rest in green meadows; he leads me beside peaceful streams. PSALM 23:1-2

Ernest

"Intent on purpose" (Teutonic)

"If you look for me in earnest, you will find me when you seek me. I will be found by you," says the LORD. JEREMIAH 29:13-14

Ethan
"Strength, permanence, firmness" (Hebrew)

"See, God has come to save me. I will trust in him and not be afraid. The LORD GOD is my strength and my song; he has become my salvation." ISAIAH 12:2

Eugene
"Well-born" (Greek)

But you are not like that, for you are a chosen people. You are a kingdom of priests, God's holy nation, his very own possession. This is so you can show others the goodness of God, for he called you out of the darkness into his wonderful light.

1 PETER 2:9

Evan
Welsh form of John, which means "God is gracious" (Hebrew).

May the LORD smile on you and be gracious to you.

NUMBERS 6:25

Faith
"Belief in God" (Latin)

I will sacrifice a voluntary offering to you; I will praise your name, O LORD, for it is good. PSALM 54:6

Felicia
"Happy" (Latin)

Happy are people of integrity, who follow the law of the LORD.

PSALM 119:1

Francis
"A Frank" (Latin)

When I learn your righteous laws, I will thank you by living as I should! PSALM 119:7

Francisco
Spanish form of Francis.

When I learn your righteous laws, I will thank you by living as I should! PSALM 119:7

Frank
"Free man" (Old French)

So Christ has really set us free. Now make sure that you stay free, and don't get tied up again in slavery to the law.
GALATIANS 5:1

Franklin
"A free landowner" (Middle English)

So Christ has really set us free. Now make sure that you stay free, and don't get tied up again in slavery to the law.
GALATIANS 5:1

Frederick
"Peaceful ruler" (Old German)

So be strong and take courage, all you who put your hope in the LORD! PSALM 31:24

Gabriel / Gabrielle
"God is my strength" (Hebrew)

The Sovereign LORD is my strength! He will make me as surefooted as a deer and bring me safely over the mountains.
HABAKKUK 3:19

Gabriela
"God is my strength" (Hebrew)

The Sovereign LORD is my strength! He will make me as surefooted as a deer and bring me safely over the mountains.
HABAKKUK 3:19

Gage
"Fixed measure" (Old Norman French)

But remember that the temptations that come into your life are no different from what others experience. And God is faithful. He will keep the temptation from becoming so strong that you can't stand up against it. When you are tempted, he will show you a way out so that you will not give in to it.
1 CORINTHIANS 10:13

Garrett
"Spear champion" (Anglo-Saxon)

So be strong and take courage, all you who put your hope in the LORD! PSALM 31:24

Gary
"Spear carrier" (Germanic)

As for God, his way is perfect. All the LORD's promises prove true. He is a shield for all who look to him for protection.
PSALM 18:30

Gavin
"White hawk" (Scots Gaelic)

Purify me from my sins, and I will be clean; wash me, and I will be whiter than snow. PSALM 51:7

George
"Farmer" (Greek)

For God is the one who gives seed to the farmer and then bread to eat. In the same way, he will give you many opportunities to do good, and he will produce a great harvest of generosity in you. 2 CORINTHIANS 9:10

Gerald
"He who rules by the sword" (Germanic)

So be strong and take courage, all you who put your hope in the LORD! PSALM 31:24

Gina
Form of Eugenia, which means "the well-born" (Greek).

But you are not like that, for you are a chosen people. You are a kingdom of priests, God's holy nation, his very own possession. This is so you can show others the goodness of God, for he called you out of the darkness into his wonderful light. 1 PETER 2:9

Giovanni
Italian form of John, which means "the grace of Jehovah" (Hebrew).

May the LORD smile on you and be gracious to you.
NUMBERS 6:25

Glenn
"Wooded valley, dale, glen" (Scots Gaelic)

Oh, the joys of those who do not follow the advice of the wicked, or stand around with sinners, or join in with scoffers. They are like trees planted along the riverbank, bearing fruit each season without fail. Their leaves never wither, and in all they do, they prosper. PSALM 1:1, 3

Grace
"Grace" (Latin)

Now may the God of peace make you holy in every way, and may your whole spirit and soul and body be kept blameless until that day when our Lord Jesus Christ comes again.
1 THESSALONIANS 5:23

Grant
"Grand, tall" (Old French)

Give honor to the LORD, you angels; give honor to the LORD for his glory and strength. PSALM 29:1

Haley / Hayley
"Heroine, victorious woman" (Norse)

Charm is deceptive, and beauty does not last; but a woman who fears the LORD will be greatly praised. PROVERBS 31:30

Hannah
"Grace, mercy, or prayer" (Hebrew)

For the LORD God is our light and protector. He gives us grace and glory. No good thing will the LORD *withhold from those who do what is right.* PSALM 84:11

Harold
"Army power" (Anglo-Saxon)

"I command you—be strong and courageous! Do not be afraid or discouraged. For the LORD *your God is with you wherever you go."* JOSHUA 1:9

Harrison
"Son of Henry" (Middle English)

"I command you—be strong and courageous! Do not be afraid or discouraged. For the LORD *your God is with you wherever you go."* JOSHUA 1:9

Heather
"Heather" (Middle English)

You, O God, are my king from ages past, bringing salvation to the earth. You set the boundaries of the earth, and you make both summer and winter. PSALM 74:12, 17

Hector
"Restrainer" (Greek)

He will give you all you need from day to day if you live for him and make the Kingdom of God your primary concern.
MATTHEW 6:33

Heidi
"Noble rank" (Old German)

But you are not like that, for you are a chosen people. You are a kingdom of priests, God's holy nation, his very own possession. This is so you can show others the goodness of God, for he called you out of the darkness into his wonderful light. 1 PETER 2:9

Henry
"Ruler of the house" (Germanic)

"See, God has come to save me. I will trust in him and not be afraid. The LORD GOD is my strength and my song; he has become my salvation."
ISAIAH 12:2

Hillary
"Cheerful, pleasant" (Latin)

Work hard and cheerfully at whatever you do, as though you were working for the Lord rather than for people.
COLOSSIANS 3:23

Holly
"Holly," a plant with evergreen leaves and red berries, usually used at Christmastime (Old English).

"Glory to God in the highest heaven, and peace on earth to all whom God favors." LUKE 2:14

Hope
"Hope" (Old English)

How we thank God, who gives us victory over sin and death through Jesus Christ our Lord! 1 CORINTHIANS 15:57

Why do you like your name?

It isn't as common as some other names, and I like that. It was fun growing up as the only Heather in my class, being the only Heather at my job, at church, etc.
Heather

191

Hunter
"Huntsman" (Middle English)

To you, O LORD, I lift up my soul. I trust in you, my God! Do not let me be disgraced, or let my enemies rejoice in my defeat.
PSALM 25:1-2

Ian
Scottish form of John, which means "the grace of Jehovah" (Hebrew).

May the LORD smile on you and be gracious to you.
NUMBERS 6:25

Jesha
"Alive and well" (Arabic)

The LORD will guide you continually, watering your life when you are dry and keeping you healthy, too. You will be like a well-watered garden, like an ever-flowing spring.
ISAIAH 58:11

Isaac
"Laughter" (Hebrew)

You will show me the way of life, granting me the joy of your presence and the pleasures of living with you forever.
PSALM 16:11

Isaiah
"God's salvation" (Hebrew)

I will lift up a cup symbolizing his salvation; I will praise the LORD's name for saving me. PSALM 116:13

Ivan

Russian form of John, which means "the grace of Jehovah" (Hebrew).

May the LORD smile on you and be gracious to you. NUMBERS 6:25

Jack

Middle English form of John, which means "the grace of Jehovah" (Hebrew).

May the LORD smile on you and be gracious to you.

NUMBERS 6:25

Jaclyn / Jacqueline

French feminine form of James, which means "supplanter" (Hebrew).

Those who lead blameless lives and do what is right, speaking the truth from sincere hearts. Those who do not charge interest on the money they lend, and who refuse to accept bribes to testify against the innocent. Such people will stand firm forever. PSALM 15:2, 5

Jacob

"Following after, supplanter" (Hebrew). The Lord molded Jacob into a man after God's heart.

Those who lead blameless lives and do what is right, speaking the truth from sincere hearts. Those who do not charge interest on the money they lend, and who refuse to accept bribes to testify against the innocent. Such people will stand firm forever.

PSALM 15:2, 5

W hy do you like your name?

I like my name because it's unique and reflects my Scandinavian heritage.
Ingrid

Jade
"Jade," a green gemstone (Italian)

When that day arrives, the LORD their God will rescue his people, just as a shepherd rescues his sheep. They will sparkle in his land like jewels in a crown. How wonderful and beautiful they will be! The young men and women will thrive on the abundance of grain and new wine. ZECHARIAH 9:16-17

Jake
Form of Jacob, which means "following after, supplanter" (Hebrew).

Those who lead blameless lives and do what is right, speaking the truth from sincere hearts. Those who do not charge interest on the money they lend, and who refuse to accept bribes to testify against the innocent. Such people will stand firm forever.

PSALM 15:2, 5

Jaleesa
Meaning unknown

He will give you all you need from day to day if you live for him and make the Kingdom of God your primary concern.

MATTHEW 6:33

Jamal
"Handsomeness" (Arabic)

May the words of my mouth and the thoughts of my heart be pleasing to you, O LORD, my rock and my redeemer.

PSALM 19:14

James

A Latin form of Jacob, which means
"following after, supplanter" (Hebrew).

*Those who lead blameless lives and do what is
right, speaking the truth from sincere hearts.
Those who do not charge interest on the money
they lend, and who refuse to accept bribes to
testify against the innocent. Such people will
stand firm forever.* PSALM 15:2, 5

Jamie / *Jamie*

Form of James, which means "supplanter" (Hebrew).

*Those who lead blameless lives and do what is right, speaking
the truth from sincere hearts. Those who do not charge interest
on the money they lend, and who refuse to accept bribes to
testify against the innocent. Such people will stand firm forever.*
PSALM 15:2, 5

Janae

Form of Janet, which means "gift from God" (Hebrew).

*Trust in the LORD with all your heart; do not depend on your
own understanding. Seek his will in all you do, and he will
direct your paths.* PROVERBS 3:5-6

Jane

"Gift from God" (Hebrew)

May the LORD smile on you and be gracious to you.
NUMBERS 6:25

Why do you like
your name?

I like my name for
two reasons: (1) My
folks chose it for me,
and (2) it's not as
common as some
names.
Jan

Janelle
"Gift from God" (Hebrew)

May the LORD smile on you and be gracious to you.
NUMBERS 6:25

Janet
"Gift from God" (Hebrew)

May the LORD smile on you and be gracious to you.
NUMBERS 6:25

Jared
"He who descends" (Hebrew)

Commit everything you do to the LORD. Trust him, and he will help you. PSALM 37:5

Jaron
"Old man" (Greek)

"I thank and praise you, God of my ancestors, for you have given me wisdom and strength. You have told me what we asked of you and revealed to us what the king demanded." DANIEL 2:23

Jarrett
Middle English form of Gerald or Gerard.

So be strong and take courage, all you who put your hope in the LORD! PSALM 31:24

Jarvis
"Keen as the spear" (Teutonic)

"I command you—be strong and courageous! Do not be afraid or

discouraged. For the LORD *your God is with you wherever you go."* JOSHUA 1:9

Jasmine
"Flower" (Persian)

You, O God, are my king from ages past, bringing salvation to the earth. You set the boundaries of the earth, and you make both summer and winter. PSALM 74:12, 17

Jason
"The healer" (Greek)

The Spirit of the Sovereign LORD *is upon me, because the* LORD *has appointed me to bring good news to the poor. He has sent me to comfort the brokenhearted and to announce that captives will be released and prisoners will be freed.* ISAIAH 61:1

Javier
Form of Xavier, which means "new house" (Basque).

"I will show you what it's like when someone comes to me, listens to my teaching, and then obeys me. It is like a person who builds a house on a strong foundation laid upon the underlying rock. When the floodwaters rise and break against the house, it stands firm because it is well built." LUKE 6:47-48

Jay
"Bluejay" (Old French)

Look at the birds. They don't need to plant or harvest or put food in barns because your heavenly Father feeds them. And you are far more valuable to him than they are. MATTHEW 6:26

Jeanette

"Gift from God." A French form of the Hebrew John.

But the LORD still waits for you to come to him so he can show you his love and compassion. For the LORD is a faithful God. Blessed are those who wait for him to help them. ISAIAH 30:18

Jeffrey

"Peaceful land" (Old German)

The LORD is my shepherd; I have everything I need. He lets me rest in green meadows; he leads me beside peaceful streams.
PSALM 23:1-2

Jenna

"Fair one" (Welsh) or "White wave" (Celtic)

Your righteousness is like the mighty mountains, your justice like the ocean depths. You care for people and animals alike, O LORD.
PSALM 36:6

Jennifer / Jenny

"Fair one" (Welsh) or "White wave" (Celtic)

Your righteousness is like the mighty mountains, your justice like the ocean depths. You care for people and animals alike, O LORD.
PSALM 36:6

Jeremiah

"May God rise up, exalt" (Hebrew)

What are mortals that you should think of us, mere humans that you should care for us? You put us in charge of everything you made, giving us authority over all things. PSALM 8:4, 6

Jeremy

English form of Jeremiah, which means "may God rise up" (Hebrew).

What are mortals that you should think of us, mere humans that you should care for us? You put us in charge of everything you made, giving us authority over all things. PSALM 8:4, 6

Jermaine

"A German" (French)

He will shield you with his wings. He will shelter you with his feathers. His faithful promises are your armor and protection. PSALM 91:4

Jerome

"Of sacred name" (Greek)

Praise the LORD! Happy are those who fear the LORD. Yes, happy are those who delight in doing what he commands. PSALM 112:1

Jerrell

Modern blend of Gerald and Darryl.

So be strong and take courage, all you who put your hope in the LORD! PSALM 31:24

Jerrica

"Strong and gifted" (Contemporary American)

Why do you like your name?

It used to bother me that I had such a popular name, but I like it now.
Jennifer

199

So be strong and take courage, all you who put your hope in the LORD! PSALM 31:24

Jerry
Form of Jeremiah, which means "may God rise up" (Hebrew).

What are mortals that you should think of us, mere humans that you should care for us? You put us in charge of everything you made, giving us authority over all things. PSALM 8:4, 6

Jesse
"God exists" (Hebrew)

Praise the LORD, for he has shown me his unfailing love. He kept me safe when my city was under attack. PSALM 31:21

Jessica / Jessie
"Woman of wealth" (Hebrew)

"Once again you will have all the food you want, and you will praise the LORD your God, who does these miracles for you. Never again will my people be disgraced like this. JOEL 2:26

Jesus
"God saves" (Greek)

How we thank God, who gives us victory over sin and death through Jesus Christ our Lord! 1 CORINTHIANS 15:57

Jillian
"Young child" (Latin)

O God, you have taught me from my earliest childhood, and I have constantly told others about the wonderful things you do.
PSALM 71:17

Jimmy

Form of James, which means "supplanter" (Hebrew).

Those who lead blameless lives and do what is right, speaking the truth from sincere hearts. Those who do not charge interest on the money they lend, and who refuse to accept bribes to testify against the innocent. Such people will stand firm forever.

PSALM 15:2, 5

Joanna

"God is gracious" (Hebrew)

But the LORD still waits for you to come to him so he can show you his love and compassion. For the LORD is a faithful God. Blessed are those who wait for him to help them. ISAIAH 30:18

Jocelyn

"Just" (Old English)

God is my shield, saving those whose hearts are true and right.

PSALM 7:10

Jodi

"Praised"

Charm is deceptive, and beauty does not last; but a woman who fears the LORD will be greatly praised. PROVERBS 31:30

Joe

Form of Joseph, which means "increaser" (Hebrew).

The wise are known for their understanding, and instruction is appreciated if it's well presented. PROVERBS 16:21

Joel
"Jehovah is God" (Hebrew)

In the same way, let your good deeds shine out for all to see, so that everyone will praise your heavenly Father.
MATTHEW 5:16

John/Johnny
"The grace of Jehovah" (Hebrew)

May the LORD smile on you and be gracious to you.
NUMBERS 6:25

Jonathan
"God has given" (Hebrew)

May the LORD smile on you and be gracious to you.
NUMBERS 6:25

Jordan / *Jordan*
"The descender" (Hebrew). The name of the river Jordan in Israel.

"If you believe in me, come and drink! For the Scriptures declare that rivers of living water will flow out from within."
JOHN 7:38

Jorge
Spanish form of George, which means "farmer" (Greek).

For God is the one who gives seed to the farmer and then bread

to eat. *In the same way, he will give you many opportunities to do good, and he will produce a great harvest of generosity in you.*
2 CORINTHIANS 9:10

José
Spanish form of Joseph, which means "increaser" (Hebrew).

May the LORD smile on you and be gracious to you.
NUMBERS 6:25

Joseph
"Increaser" (Hebrew)

The wise are known for their understanding, and instruction is appreciated if it's well presented. PROVERBS 16:21

Joshua
"Jehovah saves" (Hebrew)

O LORD, I have longed for your salvation, and your law is my delight. PSALM 119:174

Juan
Spanish form of John, which means "the grace of Jehovah" (Hebrew).

May the LORD smile on you and be gracious to you.
NUMBERS 6:25

Julia / Julie
"Youthful" (Latin)

Why do you like your name?

You can't make fun of it on the playground, and it's common but not ugly.
Julie

*O God, you have taught me from my earliest childhood, and I
have constantly told others about the wonderful things you do.*
PSALM 71:17

Julian / Julius
"Descended from Jove (Jupiter)" (Latin)

*I long to obey your commandments! Renew my life with your
goodness.* PSALM 119:40

Juliana / Julianne
"Youthful" (Latin)

*O God, you have taught me from my earliest childhood, and I
have constantly told others about the wonderful things you do.*
PSALM 71:17

Justin
"One who is just and fair" (Latin)

God is my shield, saving those whose hearts are true and right.
PSALM 7:10

Justine
"The just" (French)

God is my shield, saving those whose hearts are true and right.
PSALM 7:10

Kanisha
Meaning unknown (African American)

*He will give you all you need from day to day if you live for him
and make the Kingdom of God your primary concern.*
MATTHEW 6:33

Kara
"Dear" (Latin)

Charm is deceptive, and beauty does not last; but a woman who fears the LORD will be greatly praised. PROVERBS 31:30

Karen
Danish form of Katherine, which means "pure."

God blesses those whose hearts are pure, for they will see God.
MATTHEW 5:8

Kari
Norwegian form of Karen or Katherine.

God blesses those whose hearts are pure, for they will see God.
MATTHEW 5:8

Karla / Carla
"Womanly." A feminine form of Charles.

Charm is deceptive, and beauty does not last; but a woman who fears the LORD will be greatly praised. PROVERBS 31:30

Kate / Katie
"Pure" (Greek). Forms of Catherine and Katherine.

When I learn your righteous laws, I will thank you by living as I should! PSALM 119:7

Katherine
"Pure" (Greek)

Why do you like your name?

My name came from a nurse who played on a radio soap opera that my mom listened to back in the 30s and 40s. I think that is kind of neat.
Karen

205

When I learn your righteous laws, I will thank you by living as I should! PSALM 119:7

Kathleen
"Pure" (Greek)

God blesses those whose hearts are pure, for they will see God.
MATTHEW 5:8

Katlyn
"Pure" (Middle English)

God blesses those whose hearts are pure, for they will see God.
MATTHEW 5:8

Katrina
"Pure" (Germanic and Scots Gaelic)

God blesses those whose hearts are pure, for they will see God.
MATTHEW 5:8

Kayla
"Rejoicing" (Greek). Form of Kay.

I will sing of the tender mercies of the LORD forever! Young and old will hear of your faithfulness. PSALM 89:1

Kaylee
"Forest" (Norman French) or "slender" (Celtic)

Charm is deceptive, and beauty does not last; but a woman who fears the LORD will be greatly praised. PROVERBS 31:30

Kaylyn
"Slender lady" (Irish Gaelic)

Charm is deceptive, and beauty does not last; but a woman who fears the LORD will be greatly praised. PROVERBS 31:30

Keenan
"Enduring" (Irish Gaelic)

God blesses the people who patiently endure testing. Afterward they will receive the crown of life that God has promised to those who love him. JAMES 1:12

Keisha
"Favorite" (Central African)

But you are not like that, for you are a chosen people. You are a kingdom of priests, God's holy nation, his very own possession. This is so you can show others the goodness of God, for he called you out of the darkness into his wonderful light. 1 PETER 2:9

Keith
"The forest" (Scots Gaelic)

Let the trees of the forest rustle with praise before the LORD! For the LORD is coming! PSALM 96:12-13

Kelly / Kelly
"Bright headed" (Irish Gaelic)

The wise are known for their understanding, and instruction is appreciated if it's well presented. PROVERBS 16:21

Why do you like your name?

My parents named me Karen Ann. I found out when I was a teenager that Karen meant "pure" and Ann meant "graceful." I've often joked since then that I'm going to spend my lifetime (as a Christian) trying to live up to my name!
  Karen Ann

Kelsey

"Warrior" (Irish Gaelic)

God is my shield, saving those whose hearts are true and right.
PSALM 7:10

Kelvin

"From the narrow river" (Celtic)

"If you believe in me, come and drink! For the Scriptures declare that rivers of living water will flow out from within." JOHN 7:38

Kendall

"Valley of the River Kent" (English). A place-name.

"If you believe in me, come and drink! For the Scriptures declare that rivers of living water will flow out from within." JOHN 7:38

Kendra

"Wise" (Old English)

Fear of the LORD teaches a person to be wise; humility precedes honor. PROVERBS 15:33

Kendrick

"Bold ruler" (Anglo-Saxon)

So be strong and take courage, all you who put your hope in the LORD! PSALM 31:24

Kenneth

"Handsome" (Scots Gaelic)

May the words of my mouth and the thoughts

of my heart be pleasing to you, O LORD, my rock and my redeemer. PSALM 19:14

Keri
Irish place-name

Dear friends, let us continue to love one another, for love comes from God. Anyone who loves is born of God and knows God.

1 JOHN 5:7

Kevin
"Handsome" (Irish)

May the words of my mouth and the thoughts of my heart be pleasing to you, O LORD my rock and my redeemer.

PSALM 19:14

Kiana
Meaning unknown

He will give you all you need from day to day if you live for him and make the Kingdom of God your primary concern.

MATTHEW 6:33

Kiara
"Clear" (Italian)

Now we see things imperfectly as in a poor mirror, but then we will see everything with perfect clarity. All that I know now is partial and incomplete, but then I will know everything completely, just as God knows me now. 1 CORINTHIANS 13:12

Why do you like your name?

I really do like my name. I like it because, even though it's a fairly common name, it's also unique because of the unusual spelling. My name has always given me a sense of my own individuality, and I'm very proud of that.
Kellye

Kierra

Meaning unknown (African American)

Dear friends, let us continue to love one another, for love comes from God. Anyone who loves is born of God and knows God. 1 JOHN 5:7

Kiersten

"Anointed one" (Swedish)

I will offer you a sacrifice of thanksgiving and call on the name of the LORD. PSALM 116:17

Kimberly

"Cyneburgh's meadow" (Old English)

The LORD *is my shepherd; I have everything I need. He lets me rest in green meadows; he leads me beside peaceful streams.* PSALM 23:1-2

Kira

"Black" (Irish Gaelic)

Darkness as black as night will cover all the nations of the earth, but the glory of the LORD *will shine over you.* ISAIAH 60:2

Kirk

"Dweller by the church" (Teutonic)

He will give you all you need from day to day if you live for him and make the Kingdom of God your primary concern. MATTHEW 6:33

Kirsten

"Anointed one" (Danish)

I will offer you a sacrifice of thanksgiving and call on the name of the LORD. PSALM 116:17

Kirstie

Form of Christina, which means "Christ-bearer."

Live in such a way that God's love can bless you as you wait for the eternal life that our Lord Jesus Christ in his mercy is going to give you.
JUDE 1:21

Krista / Kristy

Forms of Christina, which means "Christ-bearer."

Live in such a way that God's love can bless you as you wait for the eternal life that our Lord Jesus Christ in his mercy is going to give you. JUDE 1:21

Kristen

Norwegian form of Christina, which means "Christ-bearer."

Live in such a way that God's love can bless you as you wait for the eternal life that our Lord Jesus Christ in his mercy is going to give you. JUDE 1:21

Kurt

"Bold counsel" (German)

Fear of the LORD teaches a person to be wise; humility precedes honor. PROVERBS 15:33

Kyle

"Handsome" (Gaelic)

Why do you like your name?

Why do I like my name? When everything's boiled down, it's probably the fact that my parents gave me this name, and that makes it special.
Kevin

*May the words of my mouth and the thoughts of my heart be
pleasing to you, O LORD, my rock and my redeemer.*
PSALM 19:14

Kylie
Possibly "boomerang" (Aboriginal Australian)

*"If you believe in me, come and drink! For the Scriptures declare
that rivers of living water will flow out from within."* JOHN 7:38

Lacey
"Lascius's estate." A French place-name.

*Dear friends, let us continue to love one another, for love comes
from God. Anyone who loves is born of God and knows God.*
1 JOHN 5:7

Lakeisha
Meaning unknown (African American)

*He will give you all you need from day to day if you live for him
and make the Kingdom of God your primary concern.*
MATTHEW 6:33

Lamar
"The pond" (French)

*"If you believe in me, come and drink! For the Scriptures declare
that rivers of living water will flow out from within."* JOHN 7:38

Lance
"Land" (Germanic)

O God, you are my God; I earnestly search for you. My soul thirsts for you; my whole body longs for you in this parched and weary land where there is no water. PSALM 63:1

Landon
"From the long hill" (Old English)

O God, you are my God; I earnestly search for you. My soul thirsts for you; my whole body longs for you in this parched and weary land where there is no water. PSALM 63:1

Larry
Form of Lawrence, which means "laurel" (Latin).

God blesses the people who patiently endure testing. Afterward they will receive the crown of life that God has promised to those who love him. JAMES 1:12

Latasha
Meaning unknown (Contemporary American)

Dear friends, let us continue to love one another, for love comes from God. Anyone who loves is born of God and knows God. 1 JOHN 5:7

Latoya
Meaning unknown (African American)

But as for me, how good it is to be near God! I have made the Sovereign LORD my shelter, and I will tell everyone about the wonderful things you do. PSALM 73:28

Laura
"Laurel" (Latin)

God blesses the people who patiently endure testing. Afterward they will receive the crown of life that God has promised to those who love him. JAMES 1:12

Lauren / Laurel
"Laurel" (Latin). A feminine form of Lawrence.

God blesses the people who patiently endure testing. Afterward they will receive the crown of life that God has promised to those who love him. JAMES 1:12

Lawrence
"Laurel" (Latin)

God blesses the people who patiently endure testing. Afterward they will receive the crown of life that God has promised to those who love him. JAMES 1:12

Leah
"Weary" (Hebrew)

But as for me, how good it is to be near God! I have made the Sovereign LORD my shelter, and I will tell everyone about the wonderful things you do. PSALM 73:28

Leanna / Leanne
A combination of Lee and Anne (Anglo-Saxon).

But as for me, how good it is to be near God! I have made the Sovereign LORD my shelter, and I will tell everyone about the wonderful things you do. PSALM 73:28

Lee
"Meadow" (Old English)

The LORD is my shepherd; I have everything I need. He lets me rest in green meadows; he leads me beside peaceful streams.
PSALM 23:1-2

Leonard
"Lion hard" (Old German)

"See, God has come to save me. I will trust in him and not be afraid. The LORD GOD is my strength and my song; he has become my salvation." ISAIAH 12:2

Lesley
"From the gray fort" (Scots Gaelic). A residence name.

He will give you all you need from day to day if you live for him and make the Kingdom of God your primary concern.
MATTHEW 6:33

Letitia
"Gladness" (Latin)

Happy are people of integrity, who follow the law of the LORD.
PSALM 119:1

Levi
"Joined" (Hebrew)

Do what is good and run from evil—that you may live! Then the LORD God Almighty will truly be your helper, just as you have claimed he is. AMOS 5:14

Linda
"Beautiful" (Spanish)

Take delight in the LORD, *and he will give you your heart's desires.* PSALM 37:4

Lindsey
"From the linden-tree island" (Old English). A place-name.

But as for me, how good it is to be near God! I have made the Sovereign LORD *my shelter, and I will tell everyone about the wonderful things you do.* PSALM 73:28

Lisa
A variation of Elizabeth, which means "God's oath" (Hebrew).

Give me understanding and I will obey your law; I will put it into practice with all my heart. PSALM 119:34

Logan
"Cove" (Irish Gaelic)

But as for me, how good it is to be near God! I have made the Sovereign LORD *my shelter, and I will tell everyone about the wonderful things you do.* PSALM 73:28

Louis
"Warrior" (German)

How we thank God, who gives us victory over sin and death through Jesus Christ our Lord! 1 CORINTHIANS 15:57

Lucas
A form of Luke, which means "light giving" (Latin).

You have heard me teach many things that have been confirmed by many reliable witnesses. Teach these great truths to trustworthy people who are able to pass them on to others. 2 TIMOTHY 2:2

Luis

Spanish form of Louis, which means "warrior" (German).

How we thank God, who gives us victory over sin and death through Jesus Christ our Lord! 1 CORINTHIANS 15:57

Luke

"Light giving" (Latin)

You have heard me teach many things that have been confirmed by many reliable witnesses. Teach these great truths to trustworthy people who are able to pass them on to others. 2 TIMOTHY 2:2

Lydia

"From Lydia." A Greek place, *Lydios* was an ancient part of Asia Minor known for its fine culture.

I am praying to you because I know you will answer, O God. Bend down and listen as I pray. PSALM 17:6

Mackenzie

"Son of the wise ruler" (Gaelic)

Fear of the LORD teaches a person to be wise; humility precedes honor. PROVERBS 15:33

Madeline / Madalyn

French form of Magdalene, which means "high tower" (Hebrew).

But as for me, I will sing about your power. I will shout with joy each morning because of your unfailing love. For you have been my refuge, a place of safety in the day of distress. PSALM 59:16

Madison
Former surname (Middle English)

"I thank and praise you, God of my ancestors, for you have given me wisdom and strength. You have told me what we asked of you and revealed to us what the king demanded." DANIEL 2:23

Maegan
American version of Megan, which means "pearl."

God blesses those whose hearts are pure, for they will see God.
MATTHEW 5:8

Maggie
Form of Margaret or Magdalene

But as for me, I will sing about your power. I will shout with joy each morning because of your unfailing love. For you have been my refuge, a place of safety in the day of distress. PSALM 59:16

Malcolm
"Of royal blood" (Scottish)

But you are not like that, for you are a chosen people. You are a kingdom of priests, God's holy nation, his very own possession. This is so you can show others the goodness of God, for he called you out of the darkness into his wonderful light. 1 PETER 2:9

Mallory
"The unlucky one" (Old French)

But as for me, how good it is to be near God! I have made the Sovereign LORD my shelter, and I will tell everyone about the wonderful things you do. PSALM 73:28

Mandy
"Deserving of love" (Latin)

Dear friends, let us continue to love one another, for love comes from God. Anyone who loves is born of God and knows God.
1 JOHN 4:7

Manuel / Manuelle
Spanish form of Immanuel, which means "God is with us" (Hebrew).

For I can do everything with the help of Christ who gives me the strength I need. PHILIPPIANS 4:13

Marcus
Form of Mark, which means "warlike one" (Latin).

Give honor to the LORD, you angels; give honor to the LORD for his glory and strength. PSALM 29:1

Margaret
"Pearl"

God blesses those whose hearts are pure, for they will see God.
MATTHEW 5:8

Maria / Marie
Forms of Mary, which means "bitter" (Hebrew).

I will offer you a sacrifice of thanksgiving and call on the name of the LORD. PSALM 116:17

Mariah
"Bitter" (Hebrew). A form of Mary.

I will offer you a sacrifice of thanksgiving and call on the name of the LORD. PSALM 116:17

Mario

Italian form of Latin Marius, which means "martial," from Mars, the god of war.

"I command you—be strong and courageous! Do not be afraid or discouraged. For the LORD *your God is with you wherever you go."* JOSHUA 1:9

Marisa

"Sea-born" (Latin)

"If you believe in me, come and drink! For the Scriptures declare that rivers of living water will flow out from within." JOHN 7:38

Mark / Marc

"Warlike one" (Latin)

Give honor to the LORD, *you angels; give honor to the* LORD *for his glory and strength.* PSALM 29:1

Marquise / Marquise

"Count of a borderland" (English and French title)

But you are not like that, for you are a chosen people. You are a kingdom of priests, God's holy nation, his very own possession. This is so you can show others the goodness of God, for he called you out of the darkness into his wonderful light.

1 PETER 2:9

Marshall

"Horse groom" (Old French)

Work hard and cheerfully at whatever you do, as though you were working for the Lord rather than for people. COLOSSIANS 3:23

Martha
"Lady, mistress" (Aramean)

Fear of the LORD teaches a person to be wise; humility precedes honor. PROVERBS 15:33

Martin
"Warlike one" (Latin)

Give honor to the LORD, you angels; give honor to the LORD for his glory and strength. PSALM 29:1

Marvin
"The sea" (English)

Your righteousness is like the mighty mountains, your justice like the ocean depths. You care for people and animals alike, O LORD. PSALM 36:6

Mary
"Bitter" (Hebrew)

I will offer you a sacrifice of thanksgiving and call on the name of the LORD. PSALM 116:17

Mason
"A stonecutter" (Old French)

Work hard and cheerfully at whatever you do, as though you were working for the Lord rather than for people. COLOSSIANS 3:23

Why do you like your name?

I didn't like it when I was young because it seemed so simple, but now I have come to appreciate it because I was named after my grandmother.
Mary

221

Matthew

"Gift of God" (Hebrew)

May the LORD smile on you and be gracious to you.

NUMBERS 6:25

Maurice

"A Moor" or "dark-skinned" (Latin)

Darkness as black as night will cover all the nations of the earth, but the glory of the LORD will shine over you. ISAIAH 60:2

Max

"The greatest" (Latin), from Maximilian.

Such people will not be overcome by evil circumstances. Those who are righteous will be long remembered. They do not fear bad news; they confidently trust the LORD to care for them.

PSALM 112:6-7

Maxwell

"From Maccus's spring or pool" (Anglo-Saxon)

The LORD is my shepherd; I have everything I need. He lets me rest in green meadows; he leads me beside peaceful streams.

PSALM 23:1-2

Megan

Welsh form of Margaret, which means "Pearl"

God blesses those whose hearts are pure, for they will see God.

MATTHEW 5:8

Melanie

"Dark, black" (Greek)

*Darkness as black as night will cover all the nations of the earth,
but the glory of the* LORD *will shine over you.*
ISAIAH 60:2

Melissa
"Honey" (Greek)

*How sweet are your words to my taste; they are sweeter than
honey. Your commandments give me understanding; no wonder I
hate every false way of life.* PSALM 119:103-104

Melody
"Choral singing" (Greek)

Come, let us sing to the LORD*! Let us give a joyous shout to the
rock of our salvation!* PSALM 95:1

Melvin
"Gentle chief" (Irish Gaelic)

*So be strong and take courage, all you who put your hope in the
LORD!* PSALM 31:24

Mercedes
"Mercies" (Spanish)

The LORD *is merciful and gracious; he is slow to get angry and
full of unfailing love.* PSALM 103:8

Meredith
"Great lord" (Welsh)

Fear of the LORD *teaches a person to be wise; humility precedes
honor.* PROVERBS 15:33

Mia

"My, mine" (Italian) or a Swedish form of Mary.

And so, dear Christian friends, I plead with you to give your bodies to God. Let them be a living and holy sacrifice—the kind he will accept. When you think of what he has done for you, is this too much to ask? ROMANS 12:1

Micah

"Who is like God?" (Hebrew)

Spend your time and energy in training yourself for spiritual fitness. Physical exercise has some value, but spiritual exercise is much more important, for it promises a reward in both this life and the next. 1 TIMOTHY 4:7-8

Michael / *Michael*

"Who is like God?" (Hebrew)

I believe in your commands; now teach me good judgment and knowledge. PSALM 119:66

Michaela

"Who is like the Lord?" An English feminine form of Michael.

Spend your time and energy in training yourself for spiritual fitness. Physical exercise has some value, but spiritual exercise is much more important, for it promises a reward in both this life and the next. 1 TIMOTHY 4:7-8

Michelle

"Who is like the Lord?" French feminine form of Michael.

Spend your time and energy in training yourself for spiritual

fitness. Physical exercise has some value, but spiritual exercise is much more important, for it promises a reward in both this life and the next.
1 TIMOTHY 4:7-8

Miguel
Spanish form of Michael, which means "Who is like God?" (Hebrew).

I believe in your commands; now teach me good judgment and knowledge. PSALM 119:66

Miles
"Merciful" (Slavic) or "soldier" (Latin)

So be strong and take courage, all you who put your hope in the LORD! PSALM 31:24

Miranda
"Admirable" (Latin)

Charm is deceptive, and beauty does not last; but a woman who fears the LORD *will be greatly praised.* PROVERBS 31:30

Misty
"Covered in mist" (Old English)

Now we see things imperfectly as in a poor mirror, but then we will see everything with perfect clarity. All that I know now is partial and incomplete, but then I will know everything completely, just as God knows me now. 1 CORINTHIANS 13:12

Mitchell
"Who is like God?" (Hebrew). A form of Michael.

Why do you like your name?

I like my name because my dad picked it—he liked the Beatles' song "Michelle."
Michelle

I believe in your commands; now teach me good judgment and knowledge. PSALM 119:66

Molly
Form of Mary, which means "bitter" (Hebrew).

I will offer you a sacrifice of thanksgiving and call on the name of the LORD. PSALM 116:17

Monica
"Counselor" (Latin)

For the LORD grants wisdom! From his mouth come knowledge and understanding. PROVERBS 2:6

Monique
French form of Monica, which means "counselor" (Latin).

For the LORD grants wisdom! From his mouth come knowledge and understanding. PROVERBS 2:6

Morgan / Morgan
"Man from the sea's edge" (Welsh)

Your righteousness is like the mighty mountains, your justice like the ocean depths. You care for people and animals alike, O LORD. PSALM 36:6

Nancy
"Woman of grace" (Hebrew)

Now may the God of peace make you holy in every way, and may your whole spirit and soul and body be kept blameless until that day when our Lord Jesus Christ comes again. 1 THESSALONIANS 5:23

Naomi
"Pleasant" (Hebrew)

Kind words are like honey—sweet to the soul and healthy for the body. PROVERBS 16:24

Natalie/Natasha
"She who is born at Christmas" (Latin)

"Glory to God in the highest heaven, and peace on earth to all whom God favors." LUKE 2:14

Nathan
"Gift of God" (Hebrew)

But the LORD still waits for you to come to him so he can show you his love and compassion. For the LORD is a faithful God. Blessed are those who wait for him to help them. ISAIAH 30:18

Nathaniel
"Gift of the Lord" (Hebrew)

"But you are my witnesses, O Israel!" says the LORD. "And you are my servant. You have been chosen to know me, believe in me, and understand that I alone am God. There is no other God; there never has been and never will be."
ISAIAH 43:10

Neil / Niel / Nils
"Champion" (Scandinavian)

Remember that in a race everyone runs, but only one person gets the prize. You also must run in such a way that you will

*W*hy do you like your name?

I've always liked my name because I was named after my two grandmothers: Natalie from my Turkish grandmother and Charlotte from my Swedish grandmother.
Natalie Charlotte

227

win. All athletes practice strict self-control. They do it to win a
prize that will fade away, but we do it for an eternal prize.
1 CORINTHIANS 9:24-25

Nicholas
"The people triumph" (Greek)
God is my shield, saving those whose hearts are true and right.
PSALM 7:10

Nicole
"Victory of the people." French feminine form of Nicholas.
God is my shield, saving those whose hearts are true and right.
PSALM 7:10

Nikki
Form of Nicole, which means "victory of the people." Greek
feminine form of Nicholas.
God is my shield, saving those whose hearts are true and right.
PSALM 7:10

Nina
"Gracious" (Hebrew)
May the LORD smile on you and be gracious to you.
NUMBERS 6:25

Noah
"Peace" (Hebrew)
The LORD is my shepherd; I have everything I need. He lets me
rest in green meadows; he leads me beside peaceful streams.
PSALM 23:1-2

Olivia / **Oliver**
"Olive tree," a symbol of peace (Latin)

Oh, the joys of those who do not follow the advice of the wicked, or stand around with sinners, or join in with scoffers. They are like trees planted along the riverbank, bearing fruit each season without fail. Their leaves never wither, and in all they do, they prosper. PSALM 1:1, 3

Oscar /Oskar
"Spear of God" (Scandinavian)

For I can do everything with the help of Christ who gives me the strength I need. PHILIPPIANS 4:13

Paige
"Attendant" (Old English)

Sing about the glory of his name! Tell the world how glorious he is. PSALM 66:2

Pamela
"Sweet as honey" (Greek)

How sweet are your words to my taste; they are sweeter than honey. Your commandments give me understanding; no wonder I hate every false way of life. PSALM 119:103-104

Parker
"Gamekeeper" (Old English)

Work hard and cheerfully at whatever you do, as though you were working for the Lord rather than for people.
COLOSSIANS 3:23

Patrice

French form of Patricia, which means "noblewoman" (Latin).

Fear of the LORD teaches a person to be wise; humility precedes honor. PROVERBS 15:33

Patricia

"Noblewoman" (Latin)

Fear of the LORD teaches a person to be wise; humility precedes honor. PROVERBS 15:33

Patrick

"Member of the nobility" (Latin)

But you are not like that, for you are a chosen people. You are a kingdom of priests, God's holy nation, his very own possession. This is so you can show others the goodness of God, for he called you out of the darkness into his wonderful light.

1 PETER 2:9

Paul

"Little, small" (Latin), signifying dependence on God.

But as for me, how good it is to be near God! I have made the Sovereign LORD my shelter, and I will tell everyone about the wonderful things you do. PSALM 73:28

Peter

"Rock" (Greek)

Wait patiently for the LORD. Be brave and courageous. Yes, wait patiently for the LORD. PSALM 27:14

Philip
"Lover of horses" (Greek)

He will give you all you need from day to day if you live for him and make the Kingdom of God your primary concern.
MATTHEW 6:33

Porsha / Portia
Roman clan name of unknown meaning

He will give you all you need from day to day if you live for him and make the Kingdom of God your primary concern.
MATTHEW 6:33

Preston
"Town of the priest" (Old English)

"See, God has come to save me. I will trust in him and not be afraid. The LORD GOD is my strength and my song; he has become my salvation." ISAIAH 12:2

Priscilla
"Ancient" (Latin). A name derived from the title of a Latin clan, so called from its great antiquity.

As for me, I look to the LORD for his help. I wait confidently for God to save me, and my God will certainly hear me.
MICAH 7:7

Quentin
"The fifth" (Latin)

He will give you all you need from day to day if you live for him and make the Kingdom of God your primary concern.
MATTHEW 6:33

Quiton / Quetin
"Queen's manor" (English)

"But you are my witnesses, O Israel!" says the LORD. "And you are my servant. You have been chosen to know me, believe in me, and understand that I alone am God. There is no other God; there never has been and never will be." ISAIAH 43:10

Rachel
"Lamb" (Hebrew), signifying gentle innocence.

He will feed his flock like a shepherd. He will carry the lambs in his arms, holding them close to his heart. He will gently lead the mother sheep with their young. ISAIAH 40:11

Rachelle
Form of Rachel, which means "lamb" (Hebrew), signifying gentle innocence.

He will feed his flock like a shepherd. He will carry the lambs in his arms, holding them close to his heart. He will gently lead the mother sheep with their young. ISAIAH 40:11

Rafael / Raphael
"God has healed" (Hebrew)

The Spirit of the Sovereign LORD is upon me, because the LORD has appointed me to bring good news to the poor. He has sent me to comfort the brokenhearted and to announce that captives will be released and prisoners will be freed. ISAIAH 61:1

Randall / Randy
"Strong shield" (Anglo-Saxon)

So be strong and take courage, all you who put your hope in the LORD! PSALM 31:24

Randi
Form of Miranda, which means "admirable" (Latin).

Charm is deceptive, and beauty does not last; but a woman who fears the LORD *will be greatly praised.* PROVERBS 31:30

Raquel
Spanish form of Rachel, which means "lamb" (Hebrew), signifying gentle innocence.

He will feed his flock like a shepherd. He will carry the lambs in his arms, holding them close to his heart. He will gently lead the mother sheep with their young. ISAIAH 40:11

Rashad
"Good spiritual guidance" (Arabic)

The Spirit of the Sovereign LORD *is upon me, because the* LORD *has appointed me to bring good news to the poor. He has sent me to comfort the brokenhearted and to announce that captives will be released and prisoners will be freed.* ISAIAH 61:1

Raven
"Raven" (Old English)

Look at the birds. They don't need to plant or harvest or put food in barns because your heavenly Father feeds them. And you are far more valuable to him than they are. MATTHEW 6:26

Raymond
"Wise guardian" (Old English)

Fear of the LORD teaches a person to be wise; humility precedes honor. PROVERBS 15:33

Rebecca
"The ensnarer" (Hebrew), signifying either a snare or a firm binding, like the marriage troth.

But as for me, how good it is to be near God! I have made the Sovereign LORD my shelter, and I will tell everyone about the wonderful things you do. PSALM 73:28

Regina
"Queen" (Latin)

But you are not like that, for you are a chosen people. You are a kingdom of priests, God's holy nation, his very own possession. This is so you can show others the goodness of God, for he called you out of the darkness into his wonderful light.

1 PETER 2:9

Reginald
"Power" (Germanic)

So be strong and take courage, all you who put your hope in the LORD! PSALM 31:24

Renee
"To be born again" (Latin)

My salvation and my honor come from God alone. He is my refuge, a rock where no enemy can reach me. PSALM 62:7

Reuben/Ruben

"Behold, a son" (Hebrew)

"So if the Son sets you free, you will indeed be free." JOHN 8:36

Ricardo

Spanish form of Richard, which means "strong ruler" (Old English).

So be strong and take courage, all you who put your hope in the LORD! PSALM 31:24

Richard

"Strong ruler" (Old English)

So be strong and take courage, all you who put your hope in the LORD! PSALM 31:24

Ricky

Form of Richard, which means "strong ruler" (Old English).

So be strong and take courage, all you who put your hope in the LORD! PSALM 31:24

Riley

"Valiant" (Irish Gaelic)

Wait patiently for the LORD. Be brave and courageous. Yes, wait patiently for the LORD. PSALM 27:14

Why do you like your name?

I like the name Rick—it's short and strong, good qualities in a boy's name. However, it is a shortening of my given name, Derrick, which I don't care for too much. My parents never called me by my given name, I never went by it, and I have spent most of my life telling people that I'd prefer to be called Rick. My advice is to name a kid what you want to call him or her, not what would look good on a medical degree or on a law firm's door.
Rick

235

Robert

"Shining in fame" (Old English)

The LORD is my light and my salvation—so why should I be afraid? The LORD protects me from danger—so why should I tremble? PSALM 27:1

Roberto

Spanish and Italian form of Robert, which means "shining in fame" (Old English).

The LORD is my light and my salvation—so why should I be afraid? The LORD protects me from danger—so why should I tremble? PSALM 27:1

Robin / Robin

Medieval form of Robert, which means "shining in fame" (Old English).

The LORD is my light and my salvation—so why should I be afraid? The LORD protects me from danger—so why should I tremble? PSALM 27:1

Roderick

"Famous ruler" (Old German)

So be strong and take courage, all you who put your hope in the LORD! PSALM 31:24

Rodney

"Famous ruler" (Old German)

So be strong and take courage, all you who put your hope in the LORD! PSALM 31:24

Roger

"Famous warrior" (Old French)

"I command you—be strong and courageous! Do not be afraid or discouraged. For the LORD your God is with you wherever you go." JOSHUA 1:9

Ronald

Scottish equivalent of Reginald, which means "power" (Germanic).

So be strong and take courage, all you who put your hope in the LORD! PSALM 31:24

Ronnie

Form of Ronald

So be strong and take courage, all you who put your hope in the LORD! PSALM 31:24

Rose / Rosa

"Rose" (Latin)

If God cares so wonderfully for flowers that are here today and gone tomorrow, won't he more surely care for you?
MATTHEW 6:30

Ross

"Fame" (Old German)

"But you are my witnesses, O Israel!" says the LORD. "And you are my servant. You have been chosen to know me, believe in me, and understand that I alone am God. There is no other God; there never has been and never will be." ISAIAH 43:10

Roy
"Red" (Gaelic)

For we are God's masterpiece. He has created us anew in Christ Jesus, so that we can do the good things he planned for us long ago. EPHESIANS 2:10

Russell
"Red" (Old French)

For we are God's masterpiece. He has created us anew in Christ Jesus, so that we can do the good things he planned for us long ago. EPHESIANS 2:10

Ryan
"Little king" (Irish Gaelic)

How we thank God, who gives us victory over sin and death through Jesus Christ our Lord! 1 CORINTHIANS 15:57

Sabrina
"Goddess of the river Severn" (English)

"If you believe in me, come and drink! For the Scriptures declare that rivers of living water will flow out from within."
JOHN 7:38

Samantha
"She who listens" (Hebrew)

Teach me to do your will, for you are my God. May your gracious Spirit lead me forward on a firm footing. PSALM 143:10

Samuel /Sam
"Hand of God" (Hebrew)

The LORD is more pleased when we do what is just and right than when we give him sacrifices.
PROVERBS 21:3

Sandra
Form of Alexander, which means "defender of men" (Greek).

So be strong and take courage, all you who put your hope in the LORD! PSALM 31:24

Sarah
"Princess" (Hebrew)

But you are not like that, for you are a chosen people. You are a kingdom of priests, God's holy nation, his very own possession. This is so you can show others the goodness of God, for he called you out of the darkness into his wonderful light.
1 PETER 2:9

Sasha
Russian form of Alexander, which means "helper, defender" (Greek).

So be strong and take courage, all you who put your hope in the LORD! PSALM 31:24

Why do you like your name?

I like my name because it's an old biblical name with a great history, but it sounds modern as well.
Sarah

Savannah

"Meadow" (Caribbean Native American)

The LORD is my shepherd; I have everything I need. He lets me rest in green meadows; he leads me beside peaceful streams.

PSALM 23:1-2

Scott

"A Scotsman" (Old English)

"See, God has come to save me. I will trust in him and not be afraid. The LORD GOD is my strength and my song; he has become my salvation." ISAIAH 12:2

Sean

Irish form of John, which means "the grace of Jehovah" (Hebrew)

May the LORD smile on you and be gracious to you.

NUMBERS 6:25

Sebastian

"Majestic" (Greek)

Give honor to the LORD for the glory of his name. Worship the LORD in the splendor of his holiness. PSALM 29:2

Seth

"Set, appointed" (Hebrew)

The Spirit of the Sovereign LORD is upon me, because the LORD has appointed me to bring good news to the poor. He has sent me to comfort the brokenhearted and to announce that captives will be released and prisoners will be freed. ISAIAH 61:1

Shaina

"Beautiful" (Yiddish)

Take delight in the LORD, and he will give you your heart's desires. PSALM 37:4

Shameka

Meaning unknown (African American)

May the LORD smile on you and be gracious to you.
NUMBERS 6:25

Shanae

Meaning unknown (African American)

Dear friends, let us continue to love one another, for love comes from God. Anyone who loves is born of God and knows God.
1 JOHN 4:7

Shane

Form of Sean, which means "the grace of Jehovah" (Hebrew).

May the LORD smile on you and be gracious to you.
NUMBERS 6:25

Shanice

Meaning unknown (African American)

He will give you all you need from day to day if you live for him and make the Kingdom of God your primary concern.
MATTHEW 6:33

Shanika / Shaniqua

Meaning unknown (African American)

Dear friends, let us continue to love one another, for love comes from God. Anyone who loves is born of God and knows God.
1 JOHN 4:7

Shannon
"Wise one" (Gaelic)

Fear of the LORD teaches a person to be wise; humility precedes honor. PROVERBS 15:33

Shante
Meaning unknown (African American)

Dear friends, let us continue to love one another, for love comes from God. Anyone who loves is born of God and knows God.
1 JOHN 4:7

Sharon
"A plain" (Hebrew)

You, O God, are my king from ages past, bringing salvation to the earth. You set the boundaries of the earth, and you make both summer and winter. PSALM 74:12, 17

Shawna
Feminine form of Sean or Shawn, which means "the grace of Jehovah" (Hebrew).

May the LORD smile on you and be gracious to you.
NUMBERS 6:25

Shayla / Shaylee
Form of Sheila, which means "heavenly" (Irish).

"Glory to God in the highest heaven, and peace on earth to all whom God favors." LUKE 2:14

Shea
"Stately" (Irish Gaelic)

Some nations boast of their armies and weapons, but we boast in the LORD our God. Those nations will fall down and collapse, but we will rise up and stand firm. PSALM 20:7-8

Shelby
"Village on a ledge" or "willow village." An English place-name.

My salvation and my honor come from God alone. He is my refuge, a rock where no enemy can reach me. PSALM 62:7

Shelley
"Clearing on a ledge" (Old English)

He will give you all you need from day to day if you live for him and make the Kingdom of God your primary concern.
MATTHEW 6:33

Sherry / Shari
Variation of Sharon or Cherie

You, O God, are my king from ages past, bringing salvation to the earth. You set the boundaries of the earth, and you make both summer and winter. PSALM 74:12, 17

Sierra
"Sawtooth mountain range" (Spanish)

Sing to the LORD, all you godly ones! Praise his holy name. Your favor, O LORD, made me as secure as a mountain.
PSALM 30:4, 7

Simone
French form of Simon, which means "hearing" (Hebrew).
Commit everything you do to the LORD. Trust him, and he will help you. PSALM 37:5

Skylar / Skyler
"Scholar" (Dutch)
Blessed are you, O LORD; teach me your principles. Be good to your servant, that I may live and obey your word.
PSALM 119:12, 17

Sonya
Russian form of Sophia, which means "wisdom" (Greek).
For the LORD grants wisdom! From his mouth come knowledge and understanding. PROVERBS 2:6

Sophia
"Wisdom" (Greek)
For the LORD grants wisdom! From his mouth come knowledge and understanding. PROVERBS 2:6

Spencer
"Steward" (Middle English)
The LORD will redeem those who serve him. Everyone who trusts in him will be freely pardoned. PSALM 34:22

Stacey / Stacy

Short form of Anastasia, which means "one who shall rise again" (Greek).

How we thank God, who gives us victory over sin and death through Jesus Christ our Lord! 1 CORINTHIANS 15:57

Stanley

"Stony meadow" (Old English)

The LORD is my shepherd; I have everything I need. He lets me rest in green meadows; he leads me beside peaceful streams. PSALM 23:1-2

Stefan

Scandinavian and German form of Steven, which means "crown" (Greek).

God blesses the people who patiently endure testing. Afterward they will receive the crown of life that God has promised to those who love him. JAMES 1:12

Stefanie / *Stephanie*

"Crown." French feminine form of Stephen.

God blesses the people who patiently endure testing. Afterward they will receive the crown of life that God has promised to those who love him. JAMES 1:12

Stephen / Steven

"Crown" (Greek)

God blesses the people who patiently endure testing. Afterward

*they will receive the crown of life that God has promised to those
who love him.* JAMES 1:12

Stuart

Form of Stewart, which means "a steward" (Anglo-Saxon).

*The LORD will redeem those who serve him. Everyone who trusts
in him will be freely pardoned.* PSALM 34:22

Summer

"Summer" (Old English)

*You, O God, are my king from ages past, bringing salvation to
the earth. You set the boundaries of the earth, and you make both
summer and winter.* PSALM 74:12, 17

Susan / Suzanne

"Lily" (Hebrew)

*You, O God, are my king from ages past, bringing salvation to
the earth. You set the boundaries of the earth, and you make both
summer and winter.* PSALM 74:12, 17

Sydney / Sidney

"Wide, well-watered land." English place-name.

*Oh, the joys of those who do not follow the advice of the wicked,
or stand around with sinners, or join in with scoffers. They are
like trees planted along the riverbank, bearing fruit each season
without fail. Their leaves never wither, and in all they do, they
prosper.* PSALM 1:1, 3

Tabitha

"Gazelle" (Aramaic)

As the deer pants for streams of water, so I long for you, O God.
PSALM 42:1

Tamara / Tammy

"Palm" (Hebrew), signifying the beauty and fruitfulness of the tree.

The LORD will guide you continually, watering your life when you are dry and keeping you healthy, too. You will be like a well-watered garden, like an ever-flowing spring. ISAIAH 58:11

Tamika / Tamesha

Meaning unknown (African American)

Dear friends, let us continue to love one another, for love comes from God. Anyone who loves is born of God and knows God.
1 JOHN 4:7

Tanisha

Meaning unknown (African American)

Dear friends, let us continue to love one another, for love comes from God. Anyone who loves is born of God and knows God.
1 JOHN 4:7

Tanner

"Leather worker" (Old English)

Work hard and cheerfully at whatever you do, as though you were working for the Lord rather than for people.
COLOSSIANS 3:23

Tanya

Russian form of Tatiana, the feminine form of Tatius (meaning unknown).

Shout with joy to the LORD, O earth! Worship the LORD with gladness. Come before him, singing with joy. PSALM 100:1-2

Tara

"A crag or high, prominent rock" (Gaelic)

May the words of my mouth and the thoughts of my heart be pleasing to you, O LORD, my rock and my redeemer.
PSALM 19:14

Taryn

Meaning unknown

He will give you all you need from day to day if you live for him and make the Kingdom of God your primary concern.
MATTHEW 6:33

Tasha

Form of Natasha, which means, "she who is born at Christmas" (Latin).

"Glory to God in the highest heaven, and peace on earth to all whom God favors." LUKE 2:14

Tatiana

Russian feminine form of Tatius (meaning unknown).

He will give you all you need from day to day if you live for him and make the Kingdom of God your primary concern.
MATTHEW 6:33

Taylor / **Taylor**
"Tailor" (Old French)

Work hard and cheerfully at whatever you do, as though you were working for the Lord rather than for people.
COLOSSIANS 3:23

Terrance / **Terrance**
"Tender" (Latin)

Since God chose you to be the holy people whom he loves, you must clothe yourselves with tenderhearted mercy, kindness, humility, gentleness, and patience.
COLOSSIANS 3:12

Terrell
"Thor-like ruler" (Teutonic)

So be strong and take courage, all you who put your hope in the LORD! PSALM 31:24

Terri
A form of Theresa, which means "harvester" (Greek).

For God is the one who gives seed to the farmer and then bread to eat. In the same way, he will give you many opportunities to do good, and he will produce a great harvest of generosity in you.
2 CORINTHIANS 9:10

Terry / **Terry**
"Tender" (Latin)

Since God chose you to be the holy people whom he loves, you must clothe yourselves with tenderhearted mercy, kindness, humility, gentleness, and patience. COLOSSIANS 3:12

Tessa
"Countess" (Italian)

But you are not like that, for you are a chosen people. You are a kingdom of priests, God's holy nation, his very own possession. This is so you can show others the goodness of God, for he called you out of the darkness into his wonderful light. 1 PETER 2:9

Theodore
"Ruler of the people" (Teutonic)

So be strong and take courage, all you who put your hope in the LORD! PSALM 31:24

Theresa
"Harvester" (Greek)

For God is the one who gives seed to the farmer and then bread to eat. In the same way, he will give you many opportunities to do good, and he will produce a great harvest of generosity in you. 2 CORINTHIANS 9:10

Thomas
"Twin" (Hebrew)

O God, you are my God; I earnestly search for you. My soul thirsts for you; my whole body longs for you in this parched and weary land where there is no water. PSALM 63:1

Tia
"Aunt" (Spanish)

His unchanging plan has always been to adopt us into his own family by bringing us to himself through Jesus Christ. And this gave him great pleasure. EPHESIANS 1:5

Tiana

Native American form of Diana, Roman goddess of the moon.

His dynasty will go on forever; his throne is as secure as the sun, as eternal as the moon, my faithful witness in the sky!
PSALM 89:36-37

Tiara

"Headdress, jeweled coronet" (Greek)

When that day arrives, the LORD their God will rescue his people, just as a shepherd rescues his sheep. They will sparkle in his land like jewels in a crown. How wonderful and beautiful they will be! The young men and women will thrive on the abundance of grain and new wine. ZECHARIAH 9:16-17

Tierra

"Earth" (Spanish)

You, O God, are my king from ages past, bringing salvation to the earth. You set the boundaries of the earth, and you make both summer and winter. PSALM 74:12, 17

Tiffany

"Revelation of God" (Greek)

I will sing to the LORD because he has been so good to me.
PSALM 13:6

Timothy
"Honored of God" (Greek)

Praise the LORD, I tell myself; O LORD my God, how great you are! You are robed with honor and with majesty. PSALM 104:1

Tina
"Little one" (Latin)

Now may the God of peace make you holy in every way, and may your whole spirit and soul and body be kept blameless until that day when our Lord Jesus Christ comes again.
1 THESSALONIANS 5:23

Todd
"Fox" (Old English)

Trust in the LORD with all your heart; do not depend on your own understanding. Seek his will in all you do, and he will direct your paths. PROVERBS 3:5-6

Tommy
Form of Thomas, which means "twin" (Hebrew).

O God, you are my God; I earnestly search for you. My soul thirsts for you; my whole body longs for you in this parched and weary land where there is no water. PSALM 63:1

Toni / Tony
Forms of Antonia and Anthony, which mean "priceless" (Latin).

God saved you by his special favor when you believed. And you can't take credit for this; it is a gift from God. EPHESIANS 2:8

Tonya
"Wonderful beyond praise" (Latin)

O Lord, you have examined my heart and know everything about me. Such knowledge is too wonderful for me, too great for me to know! PSALM 139:1, 6

Tori
Short form of Victoria, which means "the victorious" (Latin).

I will sing of the tender mercies of the Lord forever! Young and old will hear of your faithfulness. PSALM 89:1

Tracy
"Fighter" (Gaelic)

How we thank God, who gives us victory over sin and death through Jesus Christ our Lord! 1 CORINTHIANS 15:57

Travis
"At the crossing" (French)

Your word is a lamp for my feet and a light for my path. PSALM 119:105

Trent / Trenton
"Torrent" (Latin)

O Lord, I have longed for your salvation, and your law is my delight. PSALM 119:174

Trevor
"Great house" (Cornish)

"I will show you what it's like when someone comes to me, listens

to my teaching, and then obeys me. It is like a person who builds a house on a strong foundation laid upon the underlying rock. When the floodwaters rise and break against the house, it stands firm because it is well built." LUKE 6:47-48

Trey
"Three" (Latin)

"But you are my witnesses, O Israel!" says the LORD. "And you are my servant. You have been chosen to know me, believe in me, and understand that I alone am God. There is no other God; there never has been and never will be." ISAIAH 43:10

Trisha
Form of Patricia, which means "noblewoman" (Latin).

Fear of the LORD teaches a person to be wise; humility precedes honor. PROVERBS 15:33

Tristan / Tristan
"Tumult, loud noise" (Celtic)

Praise the LORD! Praise God in his heavenly dwelling; praise him in his mighty heaven! Praise him with a clash of cymbals; praise him with loud clanging cymbals. PSALM 150:1, 5

Troy
Ancient city made famous by the Trojan War (Old French).

"I command you—be strong and courageous! Do not be afraid or discouraged. For the LORD your God is with you wherever you go." JOSHUA 1:9

Ty
Form of Tyler or Tyrone

Work hard and cheerfully at whatever you do, as though you were working for the Lord rather than for people.
COLOSSIANS 3:23

Tyler
"Tile maker" (Old English and French)

Work hard and cheerfully at whatever you do, as though you were working for the Lord rather than for people.
COLOSSIANS 3:23

Tyrone
"Owen's territory" (Irish Gaelic)

Work hard and cheerfully at whatever you do, as though you were working for the Lord rather than for people.
COLOSSIANS 3:23

Tyson
"Firebrand" (Old French)

O LORD, I have longed for your salvation, and your law is my delight. PSALM 119:174

Valerie
"Strong" (Latin)

So be strong and take courage, all you who put your hope in the LORD! PSALM 31:24

Vanessa
"Butterfly" (Greek)

255

Don't copy the behavior and customs of this world, but let God transform you into a new person by changing the way you think. Then you will know what God wants you to do, and you will know how good and pleasing and perfect his will really is.
ROMANS 12:2

Veronica
"True image" (Latin)

Now we see things imperfectly as in a poor mirror, but then we will see everything with perfect clarity. All that I know now is partial and incomplete, but then I will know everything completely, just as God knows me now. 1 CORINTHIANS 13:12

Victor
"Conqueror" (Latin)

Remember that in a race everyone runs, but only one person gets the prize. You also must run in such a way that you will win. All athletes practice strict self-control. They do it to win a prize that will fade away, but we do it for an eternal prize.
1 CORINTHIANS 9:24-25

Victoria
"The victorious" (Latin)

I will sing of the tender mercies of the LORD forever! Young and old will hear of your faithfulness. PSALM 89:1

Vincent
"Conquering" (Latin)

Remember that in a race everyone runs, but only one person gets the prize. You also must run in such a way that you will win. All

athletes practice strict self-control. They do it to win a prize that will fade away, but we do it for an eternal prize.
1 CORINTHIANS 9:24-25

Virginia
"A maiden" (Latin)

Happy are people of integrity, who follow the law of the LORD.
PSALM 119:1

Wade
"To go" (Old English)

"When the Holy Spirit has come upon you, you will receive power and will tell people about me everywhere—in Jerusalem, throughout Judea, in Samaria, and to the ends of the earth."
ACTS 1:8

Walter
"Powerful ruler" (Old German)

See, God has come to save me. I will trust in him and not be afraid. The LORD GOD is my strength and my song; he has become my salvation. ISAIAH 12:2

Warren
"Protective friend" (Germanic)

There are "friends" who destroy each other, but a real friend sticks closer than a brother. PROVERBS 18:24

Wayne
"Wagon" (Old English)

I follow close behind you; your strong right hand holds me securely. PSALM 63:8

Wendy

Originated by Peter Pan author James Barrie, who gave this name to his heroine. It means friend, because a friend of his referred to him as her "fwendy."

There are "friends" who destroy each other, but a real friend sticks closer than a brother. PROVERBS 18:24

Wesley

"West meadow" (Old English)

The LORD is my shepherd; I have everything I need. He lets me rest in green meadows; he leads me beside peaceful streams. PSALM 23:1-2

Weston

"West farm" (Old English)

For God is the one who gives seed to the farmer and then bread to eat. In the same way, he will give you many opportunities to do good, and he will produce a great harvest of generosity in you. 2 CORINTHIANS 9:10

Whitley

"White glade" (Middle English)

Purify me from my sins, and I will be clean; wash me, and I will be whiter than snow. PSALM 51:7

Whitney

"White island" (Old English)

Purify me from my sins, and I will be clean; wash me, and I will be whiter than snow. PSALM 51:7

William / Willie
"The determined guardian" (Teutonic)

But as for me, how good it is to be near God! I have made the Sovereign LORD my shelter, and I will tell everyone about the wonderful things you do. PSALM 73:28

Xavier
"New house" (Basque)

"I will show you what it's like when someone comes to me, listens to my teaching, and then obeys me. It is like a person who builds a house on a strong foundation laid upon the underlying rock. When the floodwaters rise and break against the house, it stands firm because it is well built." LUKE 6:47-48

Yesenia
Tribal name (African)

He will give you all you need from day to day if you live for him and make the Kingdom of God your primary concern.
MATTHEW 6:33

Zachariah / Zachary
"The Lord has remembered" (Hebrew)

Show me your unfailing love in wonderful ways. You save with your strength those who seek refuge from their enemies.
PSALM 17:7